NURSE Entrepreneurship

The Art of Running Your Own Business

by

Adrianne E. Avillion, D.Ed., RN

CREATIVE
HEALTH CARE
MANAGEMENT

CREATIVE

HEALTH CARE

MANAGEMENT

For permission and ordering information, write to:

Creative Health Care Management, Inc.
1701 American Blvd. East, Suite 1
Minneapolis, MN 55425
chcm@chcm.com
or call: 800.728.7766 or 952.854.9015
www.chcm.com

Contents

Foreword

Owning your own small business is one of the most exhilarating, frightening, stimulating, exhausting, and ultimately, rewarding challenges you'll ever take on. As a nurse entrepreneur, you'll experience all of these emotions and more—sometimes on a daily basis! To be successful on your own, you must be a dreamer, a risk taker, and a confident professional.

There are numerous lengthy books available on starting a small business and pursuing entrepreneurship. What makes this book unique is that it was written by a nurse entrepreneur as a succinct though comprehensive, user-friendly guide for nurses who desire to own and operate their own businesses, set their own standards, and provide the quality of service they previously have only dreamed about.

I hope that you find this publication helpful on your entrepreneurial journey. I wish you success, happiness, and luck as you prepare to assume the role of nurse entrepreneur!

—*Adrianne E. Avillion, D.Ed., RN*
President, AEA Consulting
York, PA

Unit One

OPPORTUNITIES IN NURSING ENTREPRENEURSHIP

ONE

The Realities of Becoming an Entrepreneur

WHAT *IS* AN ENTREPRENEUR?

An entrepreneur is a dreamer, a risk taker, and an innovator. An entrepreneur is someone with a drive to succeed and the ability to persist in the face of adversity. As an entrepreneur, you will make your particular dream a reality.

Webster's New World dictionary defines an entrepreneur as someone who "organizes and manages a business undertaking, assuming risk in the pursuit of profit." There are many ways of pursuing entrepreneurship. You can be a full-time or part-time entrepreneur, work as a solo practitioner, or go into partnership with other entrepreneurs. But what all entrepreneurs have in common are the courage and the determination to pursue an independent career path that can carry along with it significant risks and stressors such as lack of financial security (at least in the beginning stages of business development) and exhaustive time demands. You'll probably work longer hours than you ever have before as you carve out your niche as an entrepreneur. It takes a lot of time, energy, and effort to establish a successful business.

Characteristics of a Successful Entrepreneur

There are many characteristics of a successful entrepreneur. If you are considering becoming an entrepreneur, ask yourself whether the following statements describe you and your abilities.

- I am a self-starter. I don't need anyone else to make me "get going" and keep going.
- I am highly motivated.
- I am ready to work as hard as—or harder than—I have ever worked in my life!
- I have confidence in myself and in my ability to make my dream a reality.
- I accept new ideas easily.
- I treat other people's ideas with respect.
- I have enough money to make ends meet while I get my business started.
- I am a very organized person.
- I am able to make decisions without difficulty.
- I can solve problems and overcome obstacles.
- I am flexible and adapt readily to change.
- I can instigate, sustain, and adapt to change.
- I am a good communicator.
- I am reliable.
- I am good at managing details.
- I am not deterred by setbacks.

There are always barriers and challenges to face as an entrepreneur. For this reason, the most important characteristics of an entrepreneur may be persistence, a drive to succeed, and courage. Persistence and drive can keep you going long after you may feel like quitting. Courage helps you cope with setbacks and uncertainties. As an entrepreneur, you'll work long hours without the financial security of a "regular" paycheck. No one will pay for your health insurance, sick time, or vacation time. You and your family will make financial and time sacrifices. Make sure that your family understands that they may actually see less of you as you pursue entrepreneurship. They may think that as an entrepreneur you will have more time for leisure and family activities than ever before. However, in the start-up period (generally about three years) your leisure time will likely decrease, not increase. When faced with such challenges, take heart in this old Chinese Proverb: "The glory is not in never failing, but in rising every time you fall."

Success Strategy

An entrepreneur needs to be able to compromise. Many entre-preneurs pursue self-employment in order to be able meet their own high standards, putting themselves into position to produce products and services of exceptional quality. However, no matter what entrepreneurial path you pursue, you will need to work with and satisfy your clients or customers. Compro-mise is almost always part of any business relationship. As a successful entrepreneur, you'll determine your own non-nego-tiable standards (usually values-driven or ethics-driven stan-dards) and be able to compromise on the rest.

CHOOSING AN ENTREPRENEURIAL BUSINESS

A frequently asked question is: "If I'm going to become an entrepreneur, will I need to keep doing what I've always been doing or is it possible to start a business doing something new and different?" Experienced nurses have a wide field of expertise from which to choose an entrepreneurial business. There are advantages to pursuing a business in the field you know best. Here are some of the advantages:

- You have experience in a clinical setting and can anticipate some of the challenges and problems that may occur.
- You probably already have a network of resources and potential customers or clients in your field.
- You already have a thorough knowledge of your products and services.
- Having confidence in your own knowledge and understanding of your area of expertise generally helps to decrease some of the stress of becoming an entrepreneur.

Becoming an entrepreneur in the field in which you have always worked may be the best option since it is usually the quickest and least expensive way to start your business. However, you may dislike what you're already doing for a living. What if you're bored and longing for a new and exciting way of using your nursing knowledge and skills? If you're looking for a fresh, exciting career, then pursuing something new and different may be the best option for you.

New career paths may include options that didn't exist when you entered the nursing profession, such as designing graphics for Web sites or working for Internet companies devoted to health and wellness. If you want to "shake up" the status quo and make a fresh, innovative start, then this may be the best entrepreneurial option for you. Below are some specific recommendations to help you choose your business.

First, find a business that matches your interests. You're going to work hard at it, so you'll be much happier if you really love what you're doing! What are your special talents? Do you have a hobby that makes you feel happy and motivated? How can you combine your education, training, experience, talents and even hobbies to make a successful business? Here are some ideas from nurses who have done just that:

- Two nurses with a flair for fashion and a desire to help others, open a boutique specializing in fashion and beauty tips for women dealing with the effects of cancer treatment. These nurses are also cancer survivors and have a real understanding of their customers' concerns.
- A nurse who loves to do needlework and design stitching patterns starts an online needlework shop. She designs and sells needlework patterns with a health care theme.
- A talented nurse artist earns her living designing graphics for various health care related Web sites.
- Another nurse artist is now a freelance illustrator for medical and other health care books.
- A nurse educator who dreamed of earning her living as a writer now does so as a developer and writer of online education courses for the Internet.

- Two nurses who share a love of theater now serve as medical/nursing consultants for theater, television, and movie productions.
- Two nurses with expertise in education and long-term care now have a consulting business specializing in providing on-site education specifically designed for the long-term care sector.

Consider no limits when exploring options to develop your own business. Do what you love and love what you do!

Through research, determine not only whether there is a current need for your business endeavor, but whether this need has the potential to become a "growth industry." (For more information on conducting market research, see chapter 13.) A growth industry is one that is expected to grow significantly, and somewhat consistently, over a period of time. You can probably identify growth industries by just observing what is going on around you.

Red Alert

Before committing to an entrepreneurial specialty, determine whether or not there is a need for your business. All of the enthusiasm, drive, and determination in the world won't help you to succeed unless there is a viable market for the products and services you plan to provide.

Examples of growth industries include:

- performance coaching
- organizational development
- computer consultation
- continuing education
- technical writing
- medical billing
- Web design
- elder services
- tutoring

Why pursue a growth industry? Here is one example. A nurse duo started a successful business providing JCAHO mandatory training for various health care organizations in their geographic area about 10 years ago. Currently most of these organizations have purchased computer based learning (CBL) programs for these types of mandatory training, and business in providing live training has dwindled alarmingly. You must be alert to trends and changes in your business arena and be flexible enough to adapt to those changes. As methods of education delivery changed, could these two entrepreneurs have offered other types of training to their customers? Could they have designed their own CBL training? Even a successful business can become obsolete. Make sure that your products and services keep up with changes in your business environment.

Suppose you have an innovative idea for a business that may not be considered an obvious growth industry. Does this mean that you should automatically discard the idea? Of course not! Below are some questions that will help you to analyze your business potential.

- Is there a current need for the products and services that you want to provide?
- Do you anticipate that such a need will continue or evolve?
- How many businesses or entrepreneurs are already providing the same products and services for your target market?
- What is it about your products and services that makes them different from or better than similar products and services?
- What is it about the way you plan to do business that makes you a better resource for customers?
- Have you identified your competition? Don't forget to look beyond your immediate geographic area. Consider Internet sites and mail order competition.
- How will you monitor not only what the competition is currently doing but what future directions the competition may take?

· Success Strategy ···············

Depending on your products and services, your potential market may be limitless. The Internet and other means of telecommunication have eliminated geographic boundaries.

NECESSARY FINANCIAL RESOURCES

If possible, you must carefully plan your transition from "regular" employment to going it alone. You probably know someone who has been terminated without warning. You may even have experienced this yourself. Plan ahead for unforeseen consequences. Start by developing a good business plan (more about this in chapter 9). A good plan will help you to establish your financial and strategic goals, analyze your business potential, define your customers and your competition, identify your strengths and weaknesses, and plan for growth.

Red Alert

Before putting your business plan into action you MUST answer this question: "What am I going to live on until my business shows a profit?"

If you have the advantage of time to plan and implement your transition, begin putting aside money for the sole purpose of starting your business and surviving financially until that business is established. Save enough money to survive for at least six months, preferably a year. This may sound impossible, but it isn't. Budget a set amount each month and call it your "survival" account. Pay your "survival" bill every month the same way you pay the electric or telephone bills.

Research shows that the reason many small businesses fail within the first year of their existence is because they do not have enough cash to meet their expenses. Your survival account will pay your personal living expenses such as mortgage payments, food, utility bills, etc.

But how are you going to finance your business? Some entrepreneurs have family or friends who are able to help finance their new business ventures. However, many would-be entrepreneurs take out loans to finance their business endeavors. Two common options are the personal loan and the business loan.

- **Personal Loan.** A personal loan is made to individuals based on their credit rating and personal income. If you qualify for a personal loan you are free to spend the money as you like, making this type of loan very flexible. If you decide to apply for a personal loan, however, be sure to apply for it prior to quitting your "regular" job and starting your own business. Your income from the "regular" job is probably going to be higher (at least at first) than from your business. Apply for your personal loan when your income is at its highest, since this will increase your chances of obtaining the loan. Another loan option is a home equity loan. You can generally use money obtained from a home equity loan in much the same way as a personal loan.

- **Business Loan.** New businesses are generally considered "risky" since they lack a proven track record and usually have little or no equity built up. As a result, acquiring a business loan can be time consuming. You will need to share with the lending institution your business plan and may also need to pledge personal assets as collateral in the event you are unable to repay the loan. You may want to consider a small business loan financed by the United States Small Business Administration (SBA). The lending institution will have less of a risk in this instance because the SBA backs the loan. The loan is actually offered in conjunction with the SBA.

The SBA Web site is **www.sba.gov.** Its mission is to "maintain and strengthen the nation's economy by aiding, counseling, assisting, and protecting the interests of small businesses and by helping families and businesses recover from national disasters." It is an excellent resource regarding starting a business, growth industries, and financing. Take the time to explore the site as you pursue entrepreneurship.

Advantages and Disadvantages of Entrepreneurship

Despite the risks and challenges, there are numerous advantages to becoming an entrepreneur. Most entrepreneurs will tell you that being your own boss is wonderful. You choose when and where you work. If you work best early in the morning and like to have your afternoons free, you can do so! If you are a "night owl" and are at your best around midnight, you may also have that option! As your own boss, you reap all of the benefits of your hard work. The profits generated are all yours. You are also free from the hassles of work-site policies and endless committee meetings.

As an entrepreneur, you also have the advantage of being able to do what you love and to set your own standards of excellence. You can develop your products and services the way you want to. Although you will want to remain flexible enough to meet the needs of your clients, you set your own standards and monitor your own quality. This is your chance to be the best that you can be and to achieve all that you can!

Of course, there are also disadvantages to assuming an entrepreneurial role. Most entrepreneurs start out alone. That means that in addition to being the boss, you are also the chief financial officer, the secretary, and the receptionist. You will be performing a great many tasks that someone else probably did for you when you were someone else's employee.

You will need to pay for your own health insurance and set aside a significant portion of your gross income for social security and taxes. When you take time off, whether for fun or due to illness, it means no income is being generated while you are "away from the office." Don't forget such important, often expensive, necessities like personal disability insurance, life insurance, and professional liability insurance.

Another potential disadvantage of the entrepreneurial role is the feeling of isolation. You may miss the camaraderie of having colleagues to talk to, seek advice from, and take a break with. Here are some important ways to keep collegial loneliness to a minimum.

Success Strategy

The following suggestions are not only good for keeping loneliness at bay, but will help you to expand your network of contacts and even generate more clients.

- Develop a reliable network of other nurse entrepreneurs. How can you meet them? Here are a few ideas:
  - Investigate associations devoted to nurse entrepreneurship. One such organization is the National Nurses in Business Association (NNBA). NNBA's purpose is to promote, support, and educate nurses in business. The association has a Web site that allows you to explore its various offerings and benefits. Visit them at **www.nnba.net** or call 1-877-353-8888.
  - Another organization is the Nurse Entrepreneur Network. Its purpose is to help nurses who are or want to be entrepreneurs by providing networking opportunities, education and training, and coaching; promoting nurse entrepreneur businesses to each other and the general public; and assisting nurse entrepreneurs in forming collaborative alliances and providing a resource bank. Their Web site address is **www.nurse-entrepreneur-network.org**. Their telephone number is (763) 576-9570.
  - The Nurse Entrepreneur Web site is a networking and resource directory for nurse-

owned businesses and for those who are interested in becoming entrepreneurs. They can be found online at: **www.nursingentrepreneurs.com.**

- Join professional associations related to your specific business. For example if you are a continuing education consultant, consider joining the American Society for Training and Development (**www.astd.org**). Maintain membership in nursing associations that relate to your business.

- Stay in touch with colleagues from your former workplace(s). They can be a great source of support and can also provide you with referrals.

- Join your local Chamber of Commerce. Chambers usually have a wealth of helpful information for small business owners. Some even offer group health insurance plans.

TAKING THE PLUNGE: Resigning from Your "Regular" Job

So, you've made the decision to go out on your own. How do you resign from your current job without burning any bridges? It is imperative that you remain on good terms with former employers and colleagues. They may be your first customers or good referral sources. Many nurse entrepreneurs will tell you that their first (and best) customers are their former employers.

Red Alert

Do not resign or even talk about resigning until you are absolutely certain that you are ready to go off on your own!

Some organizations may be concerned about employees stealing ideas, intellectual property, or clients, especially if the employee is leaving to start a competing business. Such concerns may make your employer ask you to resign immediately, and you don't ever want to leave on bad terms.

You may want to start to pursue entrepreneurship on a part time basis while you still have the security of a "regular" job. If you do, never give your employers any reason to think that you have been conducting your own entrepreneurial business on "their" time. Never pursue entrepreneurial projects at work. Don't make telephone calls during work time or from work telephones. If it is absolutely imperative that you call someone during your "regular" workday, wait until your official break times (e.g., lunch) and use your cell phone or a pay phone.

If you've developed projects or materials at work for your "regular" job, remember that those projects and materials are the property of your employing organization. Most companies ask employees to sign an agreement about the ownership of intellectual property. Never give your employer a reason to suspect that you may be removing projects or materials that are rightfully the property of the organization.

Leave on good terms. Give sufficient notice of your resignation. Always include something positive in your letter of resignation. For example, you might mention learning experiences that were of value, and include one or two of your most significant contributions to the organization. If you don't feel comfortable saying that you are leaving to pursue your own entrepreneurial endeavors, simply say that you are leaving to pursue a new career opportunity. However, if you have an especially good rapport with your manager you may want to share your entrepreneurial dreams, especially if you hope to make your employer a future customer.

Finally, consider the following essential actions prior to submitting your resignation:

- You and your immediate family should have all annual health examinations and routine tests and procedures while still covered by your current employer's health insurance. Explore options for obtaining your own health insurance long before you resign. This is a major expense, especially if you plan to purchase an individual policy. Consider accessing a group policy through your professional associations, college/university alumni associations, or your local Chamber of Commerce. In the United States, COBRA (the Consolidated Omnibus Budget Reconciliation Act of 1985) will usually allow you to continue to participate in your employer's insurance plan for a designated period of time. COBRA requires your employer to allow you to maintain your identical group health coverage for 18 months or more at the same rate offered to other employees of the organization. To determine the cost of your insurance under COBRA and how long you are eligible for coverage after you resign, consult with your human resources department prior to your resignation.

Red Alert

Be sure to make arrangements for continuous health insurance coverage. Don't let it lapse for even a short period of time!

- Find out when your organization's benefit plans are due to increase in value or at what time you are eligible to be vested in and/or transfer a 401K or other retirement options. Don't make the mistake of resigning in haste, only to discover that if you had waited another four weeks, your retirement benefit would have increased significantly.
- Apply for a personal loan or home equity loan before you resign.
- Pay off any unpaid balances on your credit cards. Pay off or reduce the amount owed on any other loans.

Returning to the "Regular" Workplace

Suppose once you've made the move into your new solo career, you discover that the entrepreneurial life is not for you?

What do you tell prospective employers about this brief, less successful phase of your career?

Be honest. Explain what you had hoped to accomplish and why it didn't work out. Keep your information simple and to the point. If the problem was competition, you can explain that although the quality of your services was excellent, you were not able to charge as little as the competition and still earn a living. If the problem was simply that you missed the camaraderie of a larger workplace environment, say so.

Concentrate on the positive, not the negative. Stress the good points about your entrepreneurial efforts. Talk about what you've learned and the new skills you've acquired and how this makes you a more knowledgeable, valuable employee. Never blame others or let bitterness or anger show during job interviews. Ask a trusted colleague to role-play interview scenarios with you so that you become comfortable dealing with questions relating to your entrepreneurial experience.

Reactions of Family and Friends

Don't be surprised if family, friends, and neighbors think that since you have your own business you'll be able to help them by running errands for them, babysitting, etc. This is especially true for those of you who run a home-based business. Family and friends may assume that working for yourself is a lot easier than working for someone else. They may also assume that you'll be happy to help them out since they have "real" jobs. You may hear things like:

"Honey, since you're 'free' can you take my car in for a tune-up?"

"Now that you're working from home we won't need to send the children to daycare anymore. They can stay at home with you."

"I've simply got to run some errands. Will you watch the baby for an hour or two?"

"I've got to go to work. Will you let the plumber in for me? It will be such a help considering you live right next door and you're home all the time."

In reality, you'll be spending more time "at work" (even if it's in a home office) than ever before, particularly during the first three to five years of your business venture. You can't put in a full day's work and look after your children (or someone else's children) too. Neither can you work productively if you are expected to run errands, chat on the telephone, or conduct other activities for the benefit of others.

This doesn't mean that you'll never run errands during the day or schedule an occasional lunch with family or friends. But the key word here is "schedule." Schedule these activities and remember that if you go to the grocery store or lunch with friends you'll probably be working that evening and/or on the weekend to keep up with the demands of your work.

Here are some dos and don'ts to help you, your family, and your friends deal realistically with your role as an entrepreneur:

- Come up with a schedule that shows your family and friends exactly what you need to accomplish within the workweek. Tell them that even though you are working for yourself, you are still working full time.
- Explain that you will be working longer hours, not shorter hours, in your entrepreneurial role.
- Don't get in the habit of picking up your neighbor's children from school, or allowing yourself to be "volunteered" for church or other charitable committees.
- Share your business objectives to help illustrate the demands of your business.
- Stay firm, even if it causes some temporary friction among some of your family and friends. If they are truly concerned about you and value your friendship they will understand the demands of your new entrepreneurial role.

Are you ready to pursue entrepreneurship? You are if you agree with the statements in Figure 1, "Ready to Take the Plunge?".

Figure 1: Ready to Take the Plunge?

1.	I have the essential characteristics of a successful entrepreneur.	❏ Yes ❏ No
2.	I am leaving my current job because I want to pursue entrepreneurship, not because I am temporarily frustrated with current working conditions.	❏ Yes ❏ No
3.	I have a network of professional contacts that will help me establish my role as an entrepreneur.	❏ Yes ❏ No
4.	I have enough money to pay my personal expenses for at least six months while I establish my business.	❏ Yes ❏ No
5.	I have made arrangements to finance my business (e.g., personal loan, business loan).	❏ Yes ❏ No
6.	I have made arrangements to obtain any necessary loans prior to resigning from my "regular" job.	❏ Yes ❏ No
7.	I have checked on the status of my retirement benefits prior to resigning from my "regular" job.	❏ Yes ❏ No
8.	I have made arrangements for continuous health insurance coverage prior to resigning from my "regular" job.	❏ Yes ❏ No
9.	My family and I have had our annual physical examinations and any necessary/routine tests and procedures prior to my resigning from my "regular" job.	❏ Yes ❏ No
10.	I have paid off any credit card balances as well as reducing/paying off any outstanding loans before resigning from my "regular" job.	❏ Yes ❏ No
11.	I am resigning from my "regular" job on good terms with my employer.	❏ Yes ❏ No
12.	I have the support of my family as I pursue entrepreneurship.	❏ Yes ❏ No
13.	I have established goals and a work schedule and explained them to my family and friends in order to avoid non-work related interruptions to my entrepreneurial workday.	❏ Yes ❏ No

CONCLUSION

There are many reasons for pursing the entrepreneurial life. These include:

- the desire to pursue a long-held dream
- the desire for more autonomy
- the likelihood of being downsized in your current position
- the desire to set your own standards

Life as an entrepreneur is a rewarding, though challenging experience. One of the most common mistakes would-be entrepreneurs make is to assume that they will have much more leisure time as an entrepreneur. Although the advantages of entrepreneurship are many, an excess of leisure time is not one of them. You'll work long hours without the security of a "regular" paycheck. You'll need to finance your own sick and vacation time, pay for your own health insurance, and determine how you'll cover personal living expenses while you finance your new business.

Red Alert

Don't let temporary dissatisfaction with your organization force you into an entrepreneurial role for which you are unprepared!

Ultimately, however, the life of an entrepreneur can be terrific! But what type of entrepreneurship should you pursue? The remaining chapters in this unit discuss a number of entrepreneurial options. Some of these may be the right choice for you!

RESOURCES

Drake, S. M. (2001). *Freelancing for Dummies*. New York: Hungry Minds, Inc.

Edwards, P., Edwards, S., & Economy, P. (2000). *Home-Based Business for Dummies*. Foster City, CA: IDG Books.

Sortino, J., & Shelly, S. (1999). *The Complete Idiot's Guide to Being a Successful Entrepreneur*. New York: Alpha Books.

TWO

The Consultant as Entrepreneur

Increased competition, rising health care costs, economic fluctuations, and constant advances in diagnosis and treatment mean that health care organizations require staff members to possess more skills and knowledge than ever before. These same organizations may also need assistance with specific projects that do not necessarily demand the attention of a full-time or even part-time employee. Consultants are people with special skills and expertise whose services are purchased for a fixed period of time or for the completion of a specific project. The role of the consultant is becoming more and more important to the success of hospitals and health care systems.

Consultants must have documented knowledge and skills in their area of expertise as well as references from individuals or organizations who have utilized (and been satisfied with) the consultant's services. If you are looking for your first job as a consultant, ask your immediate past supervisor (or current supervisor if still employed) for a reference. Make yourself known in your specialty area by publishing, presenting information at conferences and conventions, and becoming active in your professional associations. All of these will help you to establish and maintain credibility.

IS CONSULTING FOR YOU?

Consultants must thrive on solving problems and dealing with challenges. They are often asked to analyze complex and sometimes unpleasant problems and to propose practical solutions to them. The clients who hire you as a consultant, however, may not necessarily appreciate it when you identify processes that need improvement or correction, even if they've asked you to do so. You may also find yourself entering an organization whose employees are not necessarily thrilled to have you on the premises. You may eventually be the deliverer of bad tidings, unwelcome change, and/or additional work. Consultants must be prepared to deal with a wide range of reactions, including hostility.

Red Alert

Consultants can be quite unpopular with some staff members who do not want (or fail to see the need for) changes that often accompany consultative recommendations. You must be able to cope with overt and/or covert opposition.

Consultants are often fairly isolated in their positions. Nurse consultants often work alone or perhaps with one or two others and have little or no clerical support. You may need to perform a variety of tasks (such as typing, filing, and dealing with numerous telephone interruptions) that were handled by others when you worked in a hospital or health care system.

Consultants, like all other entrepreneurs, must be self-starters, disciplined, and motivated. As a consultant you must set your own goals and objectives, establish your own schedule, and generate your own business opportunities. If you like to share your expertise in challenging environments and thrive on solving complex problems, then the role of the consultant may be for you.

CHARACTERISTICS OF THE SUCCESSFUL CONSULTANT

In addition to being highly motivated and disciplined, consultants must project confidence, capability, and professionalism. A consultant is also a risk taker. John Gendelman, in his 1995 book, *Consulting 101*, identifies essential characteristics of a successful consultant, and they have seldom been better described. The characteristics presented in Figure 2 are based on Mr. Gendelman's writing.

Figure 2: Essential Characteristics of a Successful Consultant

Characteristic	Descriptions
The consultant is highly motivated and extremely disciplined.	Establishes a schedule, working at least eight hours a day, five days a week. Even if these hours are not spent with clients, consultant uses this time to solicit business. Makes calls, develops marketing materials, and writes articles for publication. Always spends a significant portion of the workweek "wooing" new clients.
The consultant projects confidence, capability, and professionalism.	Establishes an excellent first impression whether "in person," on the telephone, or via e-mail. Maintains that impression for the duration of assignment.
The consultant is a risk-taker.	Reviews the realities of entrepreneurship and identifies personal strengths and weaknesses. Continues to pursue success in the face of rejection and adversity.
The consultant devotes considerable time and energy to business pursuits.	Discusses time commitments with family. Is able to spend the hours necessary to start a business without jeopardizing essential interpersonal relationships.

Some of these characteristics need further explanation. For example, projecting confidence, capability, and professionalism can require some effort. When meeting your clients face-to-face for the first time, dress in professional business attire. Do not overdo make-up or jewelry. If you are bringing proposals and other materials to the meeting carry them in a briefcase (not in a tote bag with "World's Best Mom" stamped across its surface).

Red Alert

Remember that the extra hours you will need to devote to your business will challenge family and friends. If you have very small children, are responsible for the care of an ailing relative, or are in the midst of a personal crisis, you should seriously consider delaying your foray into self-employment.

If you are making your first contact on the telephone, use good telephone etiquette. Speak clearly, at a smooth (not too rapid) pace, and in a pleasant tone. Address potential clients as Mr., Ms., Mrs., Dr., etc., until given permission to use their first names. If you use an answering machine to take your business calls when away from your office, record a concise, professional message that lets your clients know they've reached a savvy entrepreneur. Never allow your children to record the answering machine's greeting, nor should you use recorded music or other audio gimmicks as part of your message. Do not make business calls when children or pets are nearby. Inevitably they will distract you and your client. Carry on business conversations in a quiet environment.

CONSULTING ROLES

Your skills, talents, and interests will help you to identify and choose the consulting role that is right for you. Here are some specialties you may want to think about while looking for your consulting niche:

- performance coaching
- management and leadership development
- accrediting standards (e.g. JCAHO)
- quality improvement/performance improvement
- legal implications in health care
- ethics
- patient care delivery systems
- office management
- work redesign
- cash flow and business issues
- health care delivery design
- continuing education and staff development

How can you recognize a legitimate need for your services as a consultant? Here are some situations that often trigger the need for the services of a consultant.

- **A need for temporary technical assistance:** Most clients are not looking for new or unusual skills. Instead they need expertise in skills that their organization's employees already possess. Technical assistance is not the "typical" consulting role. Your primary role is not to solve problems, but to fulfill the role of a temporary employee. In other words, the organization needs technical assistance for a specific period of time or for a specific project. It is not financially possible to hire additional "regular" employees for this project but it *is* possible to hire technical consultants who work for a consulting fee and do not cost the organization additional dollars in terms of orientation, training, and benefits. Technical consultants need to be effective almost immediately without the benefit of extensive orientation. The advantage of becoming a technical consultant is that these types of opportunities are fairly plentiful.
- **The need for a change agent:** An organization that needs to revise its organizational structure, carry out work redesign, or identify roles for

"downsizing" may look for a consultant whose primary role is that of a change agent. This is one of the most challenging roles a consultant can take on. You are being asked to revise the way patient care services are provided, and in some cases, to identify roles and positions that can be eliminated without compromising the efficiency of the organization. Organizations facing serious, overwhelming problems may need the services of a consultant who can analyze the situation and propose solutions that may be perceived as tough on employees and are therefore difficult to implement. In this role, you will most likely experience a significant amount of hostility from staff members since the changes you instigate may mean the loss of jobs. To fulfill this role, you'll need confidence and the ability to function in a tense, possibly hostile environment.

- **The need for assistance with compliance regulations:** All health care organizations are required to adhere to a variety of accrediting and licensing mandates. Local, state, and federal governments pass laws and develop standards that affect the provision of health care. Accrediting agency mandates also have significant impact on how patient care services are provided. Health care organizations are often on the lookout for help in achieving compliance. Ongoing survey preparation and/or the correction of deficiencies are essential to an organization's survival. If you are a compliance expert you can become a highly sought-after consultant.

- **The need for resource acquisition:** Perhaps you have a knack for locating high-quality resources at good prices. Resources can take the form of equipment, supplies, and employees. You may have an extensive network of colleagues and find that you can function effectively as a headhunter for organizations that need employees with particular skills and experience.

- **The need for specialized continuing education:** Many organizations have extensive education needs. In health care there is a constant need for continuing education and training. Such needs trigger excellent opportunities for a consultant who can plan and implement effective, specialized programs. Your success will be measured by the impact your educational offerings have on organizational effectiveness.
- **The need for funding:** Periodically, organizations plan new projects that require extensive funding. If you have a flair for grant writing and a knack for persuasion you may find a successful niche as a funding or development specialist.

QUALIFICATIONS OF THE CONSULTANT

A consultant must have experience and demonstrated effectiveness in whatever fields he or she wishes to consult. Potential clients want to see that you have knowledge and experience as well as a track record of effective consultation. If you do not have a track record as an independent consultant, you can use examples from your past and present job performances. For example, if you are seeking a role as a grant writer you may be able to produce evidence that you obtained grants as part of your former role as a "regular" employee. Discuss your accomplishments and how they enhanced organizational effectiveness at your workplace.

Many would-be consultants wonder if they need advanced certification or graduate degrees. There is no single answer to this question. Consider the following points.

- Check with other consultants in your field and find out what the typical standards are for education and experience.

- Do not limit yourself geographically when identifying standards. Telecommunications and the Internet have all but eliminated geographic restrictions. Talk to your network contacts and entrepreneurial mentors about necessary qualifications.
- Specialty certifications may be an advantage in clinical and managerial consulting.
- Graduate degrees are generally considered essential when consulting in the fields of academia and leadership/management.
- Advanced education is generally considered a "plus" and enhances credibility.

FINDING CLIENTS

Detailed strategies concerning marketing to, finding, and keeping clients are presented in Unit Four. However the following list provides some points to get you thinking about who your future clients could be, as well as how you can get to them.

- Make a list of people, health care systems, and other businesses that might need your services.
- Remember that former employers, colleagues, and contacts made through committee work and professional associations are good referral sources.
- Develop a marketing pitch including a professional-looking business card and brochure that describe your services. Send these items to your network of professional contacts.
- Make "cold" calls to potential clients that you don't know but have heard about via referrals from your network and to those who have published articles and books relating to your expertise.
- Attend meetings of your professional associations and, when possible, attend their national conventions. These are excellent sources of business contacts.

- Learn to handle rejection. You may make 10 calls a day for weeks and not generate business. Then suddenly you may receive 10 requests for your services from contacts you made weeks or even months earlier.
- Be on the lookout for new clients constantly, even when you have many clients. Remember that all consulting projects come to an end; that is the nature of consulting.

PROFESSIONAL ETHICS

Prior to soliciting consulting jobs, you need to determine the ethics of your consulting business. Ethics is the code of personal and professional moral standards you use to conduct your business. It is a good idea to put your ethics in writing. Items you want to include as part of your code of ethics are:

- confidentiality
- conflicts of interest
- ownership of intellectual property
- how fees and deadlines are determined
- guidelines for accepting assignments

Do not compromise your ethical standards. This is different from being flexible or compromising on non-ethical issues. For example, suppose you are a leadership development consultant. Your client hires you to accomplish certain tasks within a fairly rigid deadline. This is possible, but you believe that you could do a more thorough job if given two more weeks. However, meeting the original deadline will still enable you to achieve necessary goals and will not affect the overall quality of your work. You and your client discuss the deadline and she is willing to give you one, but not two, more weeks. This is an acceptable compromise.

Consider another scenario. Part of your code of ethics dictates that work you do for your clients is kept confidential. Suppose one of your best clients (client A), someone you have come to like and enjoy working for, asks you to divulge information about another client's (client B's) organization. Such information is highly sensitive and talking about it could adversely affect the way client B provides patient care services. Your code of ethics demands that you maintain confidentiality and refuse to divulge this information. Though your decision could cost you client A's business, the greater likelihood is that client A will respect your ethics. After all, if you demonstrate a willingness to violate client B's confidentiality, client A will realize soon enough that you would be willing to violate his or her confidentiality too.

EVALUATING YOUR EFFECTIVENESS AS A CONSULTANT

You can evaluate your effectiveness as a consultant in a number of ways. First and foremost, did you meet the goals and objectives established by you and your client? These goals and objectives must be in writing, objective, and measurable. They should clearly identify who is responsible for goal achievement, what actions are to be taken, and within what time frame they are to be achieved. Other ways to evaluate your effectiveness include answering the following questions:

- Have you received repeat business from clients?
- Have you received consulting referrals from satisfied clients?
- Have you received positive feedback when you make follow-up telephone calls or personal visits to former clients in order to assess the long-term effectiveness of your interventions?

What happens if you and your client are satisfied with your work but staff members are attempting to sabotage the project you've been hired to complete? Unfortunately, this is a fairly common problem, and often surfaces when significant change (such as downsizing) is anticipated.

It is best to deal with these kinds of problems directly and, whenever possible, proactively. Before you even begin work, ask your client what staff members think of the proposed project. Who will likely be supportive and who will not? Ask that your client (e.g., director of nursing) be part of the introductory meetings with staff and lend his or her support to the project and to you.

Talk directly to staff members who are and who are not supportive. Solicit their questions, address their concerns, and encourage them to contribute to the consulting process as much as possible. Be honest with staff members. Don't try to "cover up" the unpleasantness of the job you've been asked to do.

If you are truly unable to defuse the negative effects of certain staff members, discuss the situation frankly with your client. Schedule regular meetings with your client. This will help you to curb problems before they get out of control and interfere with your work performance.

NON-PAYMENT ISSUES

What happens if your client is dissatisfied with your work? What if he or she refuses to pay you and attempts to break your contractual agreement? You need to be prepared to deal with this significant problem.

Start with goals and objectives. Before accepting any consulting project, make sure that you and your client have a clear understanding of what the client needs and what you will do to fulfill that need. Put goals and objectives in writing as part of your contract or letter of agreement. Never agree to accept any type of consulting work without a contract or written agreement.

Don't wait until the end of a project to get feedback from your client. Schedule specific times throughout the course of the project to meet with the person(s) who hired you in order to evaluate progress. This way you can avoid or at least diminish the likelihood of unhappy surprises.

You may also arrange to receive your fee in installments. For example, receive one-third of the fee after a third of the project is completed, the next third of the fee two-thirds of the way through the project, and the final installment upon project completion. You also have the option of including a late fee statement in contracts and letters of agreement. For instance, if payment is five or more days late 10% of the amount due is to be paid in addition to the amount of the installment. Some consultants also include a contract termination clause into their letters of agreement and contracts. Such a statement outlines the conditions that allow either party to terminate the working relationship.

If your client refuses to pay you, you must decide whether or not it is worthwhile to take legal action against him or her. Taking legal action can be time-consuming, stressful, and expensive. It is prudent to consider at the outset whether you will spend more money and endure more stress by pursuing the fee than you would by forfeiting the money.

How will you deal with clients who try to renege on your agreement even though goals and objectives were achieved, and your clients never indicated that there were any problems or concerns? If this happens, follow the preceding suggestions concerning letters of agreement, contracts, written goals and objectives, and ongoing progress evaluation. Do your best to resolve the issue satisfactorily. You must protect your income, your personal reputation, and the reputation of your business.

TURNING DOWN POTENTIAL CLIENTS

Now suppose you don't want to work for a particular client because of the nature of the project, ethical conflicts, or other important concerns. You always want to refuse tactfully and try to avoid burning bridges or leaving an unpleasant impression.

Your first step is to determine *why* you want to avoid working for this particular client.

- **Is it because you are not qualified to complete the project?** If this is the reason, say so. Most clients will respect your honesty. No matter how badly you need the work, don't accept a project for which you are not qualified. If you do, both you and your client will be dissatisfied and you will be forced to deal with the consequences of a job poorly done.

- **Does the client have unrealistic expectations?**
  For example, are there insufficient resources
  or time to complete the project? Discuss these
  barriers with your client. Perhaps you can
  negotiate more satisfactory working conditions.
- **Does the project violate your ethical standards?**
  If so, refuse the project.
- **Is the project itself inappropriate or, in your
  opinion, just a bad idea?** *Tactfully* express your
  concerns to the potential client. You may be
  able to propose other options. Don't agree to
  work on a project if you truly believe that it
  will be detrimental to your client and his or her
  organization.
- **Does the client want too much work for too
  little money?** Determine whether you can afford
  to put in the time on this project knowing it will
  produce minimal financial rewards and possibly
  prevent you from working on other projects and/
  or pursuing other clients. If you are just starting
  your career as an entrepreneur and need this client
  to jump-start your business you may choose to
  accept the job.

Success Strategy

Always formulate a written letter of agreement or contract with
your client. Make sure that these documents include goals, objectives, time frames, fees, and measurements of success.

CONCLUSION

Maintain skills, knowledge, and expertise in your chosen field.
Use your network of contacts and professional associations as
well as professional journals to stay up-to-date. Surf the Internet for pertinent information. Attend relevant continuing
education programs.

Your clients will want to know that your work reflects the most current "happenings" in the health care arena. Be prepared to answer questions about your past experience as well as how you remain on the "cutting edge" of your specialty.

Honesty is critical to your success as a consultant—honesty with yourself and your clients. Formulating your own code of ethics will help you set standards and maintain the integrity of your business.

Review the resources at the end of this chapter. Although some of them are older publications, they are based on timeless principles and will add to your knowledge base as you pursue your consulting career.

RESOURCES

Block, P. (1981). *Flawless Consulting*. San Diego, CA: Pfeiffer.

Cockman, P., Evans, B., & Reynolds, P. (1996). Client-Centered Consulting. New York: McGraw-Hill.

Forsyth, D. M., Rhudy, L., & Johnson, L. M. (2002). The Consultation Role of a Nurse Educator. *The Journal of Continuing Education in Nursing,* 33(5), 197-202.

Gendelman, J. (1995). *Consulting 101. How to Succeed as a Training Consultant.* Alexandria, VA: American Society for Training and Development.

Lewin, M. D. (1995). *The Overnight Consultant.* New York: John Wiley & Sons.

THREE

The Service Provider as Entrepreneur

Service provision generally involves direct provision of particular services combined with consulting. As an entrepreneur in service provision, you will develop and implement roles and services that involve working within or for various health care organizations.

OPPORTUNITIES IN SERVICE PROVISION

In addition to some of the growth industries mentioned in chapter 1, the following are some good specialty ideas for the entrepreneur in service provision.

- **Elder Services.** Consider the case of the entrepreneur who opened an adult daycare center for patients with dementia and Alzheimer's. Our population is aging, and numerous services are needed by older patients. The need for daycare is especially critical. Another need is family education. Family members have ongoing needs including not only how to physically care for their elderly relatives, but dealing with patients' emotional behaviors as well as how to deal with caregiver burnout.
- **Marketing.** The images of health care providers, hospitals and health systems, and health insurance

companies fluctuate wildly. Most of these entities are constantly on the lookout for individuals who can help to improve their public relations image and/or market their organizations more effectively. As a service provider you may be able to act as an effective liaison between the consumer and the client who hires you.

- **Home Health.** Health care provision is being conducted in outpatient and community settings at a rapidly increasing rate. If you have a background and interest in these settings you may have what it takes to open a home health agency.
- **Medical Billing/Insurance.** Dealing with billing and insurance issues is becoming increasingly complex. Some entrepreneurs have run successful medical billing businesses from their homes.
- **Alternative medicine and mind/body wellness.** More and more health care consumers are looking for more "natural" approaches to wellness. Unfortunately, consumers may not realize that alternative approaches, such as the use of herbal medicines, can have adverse effects if used indiscriminately. Expertise in these areas can be the seed of an entrepreneurial enterprise. Opportunities including teaching yoga, Tai Chi, stress reduction, relaxation techniques, visualization, and other meditative skills.

Red Alert

When embarking on a career in alternative medicine and/or mind/body wellness, be sure that you cannot be accused of practicing medicine without a license or violating nursing licensure mandates. Check with your state licensing board to verify what you can and cannot provide.

Consider essential qualifications when pursuing entrepreneurship as a service provider. Any potential client will expect you to have experience and demonstrated expertise. Find out what types of training and credentials (including formal education) are standard in the fields you want to pursue.

Two types of service providers require explanation beyond what was listed previously. These are the role of the manager and the role of the staff development specialist in service provision.

THE MANAGER AS A SERVICE PROVISION ENTREPRENEUR

Red Alert

If you are planning on running a business such as an adult daycare or similar endeavor, get yourself up-to-date on labor laws and personnel issues. Additionally, the laws and regulations governing independent health care agencies or other establishments that offer health-related services are numerous and complex. Obtain the services of an attorney who is experienced in business establishment to help you every step of the way.

As an experienced man-ager you may be interested in developing and implementing a system to recruit and groom managers. Perhaps you have an interest in using patient classification systems to develop more effective staffing patterns. Maybe you even have an idea for a new and improved nursing care delivery process.

Staffing is an ongoing concern for all management. You may want to establish a business that provides organizations with temporary nurse managers or directors of nursing while the organizations search for permanent candidates. You may have what it takes to run a temporary staffing agency. There will always be a need for highly qualified, skilled professionals. You may even create an agency that specializes in "hard-to-find" nurses such as those with expertise in critical care.

Perhaps you are a nurse with expertise in business plans and financial concepts. There are few health care organizations that would not benefit from additional expertise in financial management.

Health care organizations often have a desperate, ongoing need for management training and leadership development.

Because of attrition, expansion of services, and promotions, there are always staff members who, new to management, need managerial training. Experienced managers also need continuing education, particularly in areas such as labor relations and legal issues. You could offer customized, onsite training, write managerial handbooks, or development computer based training for managers.

STAFF DEVELOPMENT SPECIALIST AS A SERVICE PROVISION ENTREPRENEUR

Staff development specialists have numerous entrepreneurial opportunities. Here are some ideas for the staff development specialist who wants to be an entrepreneur:

- **Creative Training Techniques:** Making learning fun and interesting is an ongoing challenge. There are successful companies devoted to helping hospital-based staff development specialists enhance the creativity and quality of their programs. This type of business also provides excellent opportunities to market to a global customer base. They can be marketed on the Internet and have a world-wide appeal.
- **Education Specialist for Professional Trade Associations:** Many professional associations lack the funds to hire personnel for the purpose of staff development. However, all trade associations need to provide continuing education in some format for their members as well as their staff. You may be able to contract with associations to provide education for their members and staff. Remember that such associations usually have members throughout the state, country, or even the world. Think globally.
- **Online Continuing Education Companies:** A good example of a growth industry is online continuing education. You may decide to develop

such a company. Or you may be interested in contracting with these types of companies to develop educational programs for online use.

- **Train-the-Trainer Programs:** Another educational option is the development of train-the-trainer programs for persons new to the staff development/continuing education field. Many persons are given staff development positions because of their clinical or managerial expertise. However, they often lack teaching experience. Few hospital-based staff development departments have the time and resources to provide extensive orientation to new staff development specialists. They may be glad to outsource this task to you!

- **Training to Meet the Requirements of Accrediting Organizations:** This type of training is usually the least favorite part of the staff development specialist's job. Entrepreneurs have established successful businesses that offer various types of mandatory training in a wide variety of formats, including computer-based-learning (CBL). You may offer education for the purpose of preparing staff for upcoming accreditation visits and/or helping staff to implement changes to overcome accreditation deficiencies. You may find that long-term care facilities have a great need for this type of service.

- **Researcher:** Many staff development specialists have been involved in clinical research. The facilitation and development of clinical research protocols is a service that is in great demand not only in health care organizations but in the pharmaceuticals industry as well.

- **Work Redesign:** Hospitals and health systems are constantly undergoing reorganization. Facilitating work redesign and providing education and training for staff assuming new or altered roles may prove to be the cornerstones of your entrepreneurial efforts.

- **Academia:** Academia offers a variety of entrepreneurial opportunities. Here are some examples:
  - *Guest faculty:* Some academic programs frequently look for temporary faculty to "fill-in" for faculty who are on medical leave or sabbatical. Sometimes academic programs hire part-time faculty to supervise nursing students in clinical settings. You may have a particular expertise that makes you a valued guest lecturer.
  - *Faculty inservice*: Faculty members also have continuing education needs. You may offer successful continuing education/professional development programs for faculty.

The credentials you will need as an entrepreneur who specializes in various types of education will vary depending on the setting. If you are planning to offer clinically-related programs you must have the appropriate clinical and teaching experience as well as specialty certification. Consider obtaining a degree in adult education since this is the cornerstone of education businesses. Certification in staff development and continuing education is also an option.

If you want to work in academia you will need an appropriate graduate degree. In fact, since most colleges and universities require that their faculty members be prepared at the doctoral level, you are more likely to obtain work in this setting if your have a doctorate.

Some major health care systems have positions such as Vice-President for Education or Chief Learning Officer. These roles generally require a doctorate. If you plan on counting such organizations among your clients you need to explore graduate education. Talk to some educator entrepreneurs whom you respect and find out what credentials and qualifications they possess. As with any business endeavor, find out the standard qualifications and take steps to meet them.

How do you measure your effectiveness as an entrepreneur in the business of education? Initially, success is measured by client satisfaction. However, you also need to know what impact your education has on organizational effectiveness. This information may be difficult to obtain since, after your contract is fulfilled, organizations have no obligation to furnish you with additional data. These data include information from risk management findings, medical records, or performance evaluations.

Consider making a "follow-up" session part of your contract agreement. This session would allow you and your client to evaluate the effectiveness of your work together. Involving your clients in this evaluation process gives you good opportunities to solicit them as references for future clients. It will certainly help you to secure additional business if you have testimonials from satisfied clients listing how your educational endeavors helped improve organizational performance.

CONCLUSION

Service provision offers you a wide variety of ways to use your expertise and develop a successful business. You will have an opportunity to combine service provision expertise with consulting skills. The resulting business is one that offers variety, professional stimulation, and challenge.

RESOURCES

Avillion, A. E. (Ed.). (2001). *Core Curriculum for Staff Development*. Pensacola, FL: National Nursing Staff Development Organization.

Avillion, A. E. (Ed.). (2004). *A Practical Guide to Staff Development. Tools and Techniques for Effective Education*. Marblehead, MASS: hcPro.

Kaufman, K. (2000). *Finance in Brief. Six Key Concepts for Health care Leaders*. Chicago: Health Administration Press.

Marrelli, T. M. (2004). *The Nurse Manager's Survival Guide, 3rd ed*. St. Louis: Mosby.

FOUR

The Writer as Entrepreneur

Do you love to write? If so, the role of entrepreneurial writer may be for you! However, there are some unique financial implications for the entrepreneurial writer. First, you need to establish a reputation as a published author before you can even begin to think about earning a living as a writer. Write an article for a professional journal or contribute to a newsletter. These endeavors seldom, if ever, pay you for these types of publications. However, publishing in respected journals and newsletters does give you the experience and "track record" of a published author. After acquiring publication experience you will be able to pursue projects that compensate you financially for your work.

TIPS FOR THE NOVICE WRITER

Publishing your first manuscript requires a great deal of perseverance. Here are some guidelines for the would-be entrepreneurial writer who has not yet published or who has very few publications to his or her credit:

- Select a topic with which you are *very* familiar. Perhaps you've worked on a research project, dealt with a particularly challenging clinical situation, or developed an innovative method of patient care delivery. Rely on your experience and knowledge.

- Determine what journals are appropriate for the type of article you want to publish. Select a respected professional journal that requires review of your article by a qualified review board.
- Be aware that some journals receive a large number of submissions and have a "backlog" of articles waiting to be published. It may take as long as a year or more after your article is accepted for publication before it appears in print. The wait may be considerably shorter for other journals. Ask your editorial contact at the journal you select how long it takes for an article to be reviewed and how long after its acceptance it will be published.
- All professional journals have guidelines for authors. These guidelines are usually available in every issue of the journal and/or on the journal's Web site. Adhere carefully to these guidelines. If you don't, your article will probably not even be reviewed. Most guidelines ask that you submit a preliminary outline and/or abstract of your article before you actually write it. This is to ensure that you are writing about a topic that the journal's editor is interested in publishing.

Success Strategy

If a particular journal is not interested in your topic it does not necessarily mean that it is a bad idea. It could simply be that they already have a number of similar articles ready for publication. If no explanation for your rejection is offered, ask for one.

- After you write the first draft of your article, ask a colleague whose opinion you respect to review it. Don't pick a close friend. You want someone who will give you objective, constructive criticism. You don't want someone to review it who is so afraid of hurting your feelings that he or she will tell you it's terrific even if it's not.

- After you submit your article to the journal it will go through a review process. Most journals have every article that is submitted reviewed by at least two reviewers. You will most likely be asked to rewrite portions of your article. Take every suggestion for improvement seriously. Don't let them discourage you. You need to be willing to accept constructive criticism and work to improve your writing.

- Don't take it personally if your article is rejected. If and when this happens, learn from the experience and pay attention to the feedback the journal's editorial staff provides. All writers experience rejection. Just keep at it.

- Note that professional journals rarely, if ever, compensate authors financially.

- After you have a few publications to your credit, begin to look for writing opportunities that offer honoraria. Most publishing houses will compensate authors who contribute chapters to a professional text. As your writing skills improve and your reputation as a writer grows, you may even write an entire book or monograph that deals with your area of professional expertise. Be patient, however. Writing is not a career that develops overnight.

Success Strategy

Most reviewers relay feedback in an objective, constructive manner. However, there are exceptions to this rule. If you receive feedback that seems harsh or even rude, try not to be too discouraged. Learn from any points that will help you to improve your writing and ignore the rest!

PUBLISHING OPTIONS

After you've gone through the publishing process described in the preceding paragraphs, you'll want to find a way to earn money as a writer. Here are some ideas to think about.

If you have a specific idea for a professional text, contact one of the many health care publication companies and ask to speak to the editor in charge of nursing or health care publications. Prepare a written abstract as well as an outline to help you discuss your ideas intelligently. If your ideas interest the editor, he or she will ask you to send this information and perhaps an initial draft of a first chapter as part of a formal proposal. You may want to contact these editors and ask if they have any need for nurse contributors for specific books. A good way to enter the publishing world is to write a chapter for a book being compiled by a nurse editor. There is generally a small honorarium and it is good experience and exposure. Here are some Web sites of companies that publish nursing materials. (Note that Web sites change quickly. These are accurate as of this writing):

- Springer Publishing Company:
  www.springerpub.com
- Lippincott Williams & Wilkins:
  www.lww.com
- F. A. Davis Company:
  www.fadavis.com
- Elsevier:
  www.elsevierhealth.com
- Jones & Bartlett Publishers:
  http://nursing.jbpub.com

Publishing companies sometimes need the help of a content expert to review manuscripts. This type of work requires that you have experience and a background in both nursing and publishing. You will help these companies to publish work that is both accurate and interesting.

Newsletters are another good opportunity for the writer entrepreneur. Professional associations and healthcare organizations might be glad to outsource some writing projects for their in-house publications.

Online health care companies are often searching for authors to write relevant articles, do research, or write continuing education programs. There are hundreds of such companies. For an up-to-date search simply type "continuing education for health care professionals" and search the Internet for companies that interest you. The companies most likely to be looking for writers often have an "Information for Authors" section as part of the Web site.

Finally, consider writing for the average health care consumer. Hospitals, health systems, online companies, and book publishing companies may have divisions devoted exclusively to the needs of patients and their families. This takes a special talent for turning health care jargon and technical terminology into prose that the average consumer can understand.

CREDENTIALS OF THE ENTREPRENEURIAL WRITER

As in all other entrepreneurial fields, you need to find out what the standards are for writers in your areas of interest and expertise. You also need to establish a "track record" of successful publications.

Depending on the company you write for, specific academic degrees may be desirable or even required. Read a variety of different types of publications to get a "feel" for various types of writing and the qualifications of authors whose work you admire and respect.

Red Alert

You need to be a very careful financial manager if you plan to earn your living as a writer. For example, you usually do not get paid until your manuscript has been accepted in its final format. This means after you've completed all necessary revisions. This could take weeks or even months. As an entrepreneurial writer you truly need to be constantly on the alert for continued business! Additionally, companies may pay more experienced writers a higher fee because their work requires less editing and revisions.

A WORD ABOUT PLAGIARISM

Did you know that the dictionary offers the words "stealing" and "illegal use" to define plagiarism? Occasionally, an author will take portions of copyrighted work and try to pass it off as their own writing. Remember, even if you innocently use a few sentences from a copyrighted text, you are still plagiarizing and can be sued for your mistake. Here are some tips on how to avoid being suspected of using another author's work illegally.

- Reference your work meticulously. Use whatever referencing style your client mandates (e.g., APA) and strictly adhere to it. Become familiar with whatever style you use and be sure to have the most recent style reference manual in your possession. Keep this manual next to your computer for quick access.

- Remember that you will rarely (if ever) retain the copyright to a manuscript or education program published and purchased by your client. The publisher retains copyright privileges. For example, suppose you write a monograph for Company A. This company likes it, publishes it, and pays you for it. It's such a great piece of writing that you then sell the identical manuscript to Company B, who also pays you for it and publishes it. You have just done something illegal. Company A "owns" that manuscript and you no longer have the right to distribute it. That doesn't mean you can't write on the same topic for more than one company. It just means that you cannot submit a previously published manuscript—even if you are its author—to another publisher.

- Explanations and agreements about copyright and ownership of your written work are included in written contracts and letters of agreement. Review these documents carefully.

ENHANCING YOUR WRITING SKILLS

As an entrepreneurial writer, it's very important to work on improving you writing skills. Here are some continuing education options for writers.

- Take a course in creative writing, technical writing, or editing. Many colleges and universities have credit and non-credit courses on writing and manuscript development. Some high schools and public libraries also offer such courses.

- Major bookstores such as Barnes & Noble and Borders, as well as smaller independent bookstores, are often gathering places for would-be authors. Some of these individuals have formed "writers" groups and meet on a regular basis to offer support and provide constructive criticism to members. Call your local bookstores and ask if they have these types of groups. If not, consider starting one!

- Search the Internet for writers' groups that meet online.

- Contact successful authors whom you admire. Many of them remember what it was like trying to establish themselves as writers. Some may even be willing to mentor you. But be considerate and tactful. Before you ask for help, establish a professional rapport. Understand that they, too, are busy, and be respectful of their time and knowledge.

- Consider joining professional associations for writers. A good example is the American Medical Writers Association found at **www.amwa.org**. They offer extensive educational programs, employment opportunities, and self-study options.

CONCLUSION

Pursuing an entrepreneurial life as a writer is accompanied by some unique challenges. It requires not only perseverance, but the ability to accept constructive criticism as a routine part of your work life. It also requires careful money management.

The opportunity to express your creativity in writing is a wonderful way to earn a living. It allows you the freedom to pursue your professional interests while embracing a new career option.

RESOURCES

Avillion, A. E. (Ed.). (2001). *Core Curriculum for Staff Development.* Pensacola, FL: National Nursing Staff Development Organization.

FIVE

Turning Hobbies into Businesses

The purpose of this brief chapter is to introduce you to the concept of combining your favorite leisure activities with the role of the nurse entrepreneur. This may sound like a bit of a stretch, but if you have the imagination and are not afraid of risk, you may be able to turn your hobbies into successful businesses!

EXAMPLES OF HOBBIES AS BUSINESSES

- Do you have a flair for fashion and clothing design? Think of the variety of health care problems that affect how men and women dress. People who use wheelchairs for mobility need pants that are longer than if they were standing. What about people who need special shoes? How about cancer survivors who need wigs and clothing designed to accommodate various prostheses? How do people learn to apply makeup with the one unaffected arm after a stroke? There are many people who are dealing with the aftermath of devastating illnesses and injuries who would welcome help in "looking good." Body image and self-esteem are intricately linked, and you may be able to help people enhance both. The best example I know of is two breast cancer survivors who run a boutique for other cancer survivors. The boutique is a place where people can be fitted for wigs and prostheses while learning how to maintain and enhance their body images during difficult times.

- Would you like to design uniforms and accessories for health care professionals? Closely related to the previous example, this idea revolves around the need for talented people who can design attractive, practical uniforms and useful health care accessories for the health care professional. There are numerous catalogues and stores for such products. Perhaps you have what it takes to design these items!

- Do you have artistic talent? There are many opportunities for the nurse-artist. Medical illustrators are in demand for professional texts, journals, and Web sites. If this idea appeals to you, contact the major health care publishing houses for possible career opportunities. Also contact health care Web sites. Such sites are often looking for graphic artists.

- Are you an actor or actress at heart—or even by training? Consider the entertainment industry. This concept is somewhat geographically limiting, but if you've always had a yen to see your name in lights you may want to pursue a career as a medical consultant for television, radio, and theater. Don't forget your local small theaters when searching for groups that may need medical consultation. Many story lines involve health care themes and require that a professional health care worker provide expertise and advice as to the accuracy of what is being portrayed. You may also want to develop health care videos and other means of media communication devoted to health care.

- Do you enjoy working with computers? Maybe you are one of those individuals who loves working with computers and has real talent in this area. There are countless opportunities in health care for people with computer expertise. Health care organizations use computers to document patient care, record test results, track educational attendance, etc. You may be able to make an excellent living as a computer consultant.

- Are you an avid needle-worker? For those of you who love to knit, sew, and do needlepoint and other stitching projects, you may want to think about designing health care related products. I know of an entrepreneur who developed a successful part-time business designing knitting, sewing, and stitching patterns with health care themes.

- Do you enjoy building and construction projects? Do you have a talent for architectural design? Health care organizations are often in need of consultants to help design the physical plant for new services or redesign for existing services that have changed. Most builders could benefit from a health care expert assisting in the design and implementation of health care facilities.

TURNING A HOBBY INTO A SERIOUS BUSINESS

Are you concerned that a business that starts as a hobby will not be taken seriously by potential customers? If you take yourself seriously, and conduct yourself as a professional business owner, you will be taken seriously by your colleagues and clients and customers. If you behave as though your business is really "just a hobby," that is how others will see it.

When considering what sort of business to start, make sure you adhere to ethical and legal standards. For example, suppose you know about a nurse-owned business that designs and manufactures nursing uniforms and novelty items. You have some good ideas for a similar business. Is it legal to start a similar business that would target the same market? Is it ethical?

While an idea can't be copyrighted, the way an idea is presented *can* be copyrighted. If your ideas are original and not merely a "copy" of another's products and services, you are probably within your rights to develop your ideas as part of your own business. It is wise, however, to obtain legal counsel as you develop your products and implement your business. Be honest and up-front with your attorneys and business advisors. If you think some of your products may resemble another person's products, be sure to discuss that fact and obtain the best possible counsel. It's better to be cautious than to run the risk of being sued.

The prospect of developing, manufacturing, and distributing products may be overwhelming to you. If this is the case, consider selling your ideas to companies specializing in your areas of interests. For example, if you have some terrific ideas for new novelty items, contact companies who already have a business in place and offer to sell your idea to them. The easiest way to break into "hobby" businesses is to work for an established company. Just remember, once you sell your idea to a particular company, that company owns your idea. You can no longer distribute it yourself or sell it to another company.

CONCLUSION

Nurse entrepreneurs have turned hobbies into successful businesses with a little luck and a lot of hard work and imagination. Be aware that the same rules of business and ethics that were discussed in previous chapters apply to these types of "hobby" businesses as well. Turning a hobby into a business takes confidence, daring, and the willingness to branch out in a whole new way!

Unit Two

LEGAL CONSIDERATIONS

SIX

Business Structures

When starting your own business, one of the things you need to decide is what form of business—or what legal structure—you want to establish. Base your decision on what type of business you are starting and how you want to conduct business transactions.

Most home-based businesses, for example, are sole proprietorships. As a sole proprietor, you are operating your business by yourself. This means that you bear the entire responsibility for its success or its failure.

A partnership has the advantage of shared responsibilities, workload, and risks. But you also share the profits.

There are advantages and disadvantages associated with each type of business structure. The descriptions that follow will help you decide which structure best meets your needs. As your business grows and evolves, you may find that your business structure needs to change. For example, suppose you initially structure your business as a sole proprietorship. Eventually, a growing workload and increased number of clients necessitate the development of a partnership. Or you may choose to dissolve a partnership that is not meeting your needs or the needs of your partners. You must continually evaluate the effectiveness of your business structure.

SOLE PROPRIETORSHIPS

Sole proprietorship is the simplest business structure and consists of just one person who owns and operates the business. If you elect to structure your business as a sole proprietorship you will find that it is easy to establish and maintain. All you need to do is apply for an occupational business license in the municipality or community in which the business is located.

There is not a lot of paperwork or "red tape" associated with a sole proprietorship. This structure allows you complete control over all aspects of your business. As an independent and autonomous entrepreneur you select the clients you want to work for, plan strategies to complete projects, and chart the course of your business without answering to others. You keep all profits generated by your business and take all credit for its success.

• Success Strategy •••••••••••••••••

Sole proprietors MUST keep business records (e.g., income, expenses) separate from personal finance records. Open a checking account to use only for business and obtain a credit card that you use only for business expenses.

Another advantage to sole proprietorships is that they are fairly streamlined to operate. If you have no employees, you may use your social security number as your taxpayer identification number. You are taxed as an individual and don't need to file a separate tax return for your business. Your business expenses and income are part of your personal tax return, Form 1040. You attach a Schedule C form (a record of your profits and losses) to the 1040 form. In addition to your annual tax filing, you pay estimated taxes on a quarterly basis on the 15th of January, April, June, and September. You may be eligible for depreciation allowances and other deductions. Be sure that you discuss tax issues very carefully with your accountant. In fact, selecting and working with an accountant is one of the very first business actions you must take.

There are disadvantages to sole proprietorship. As a sole proprietor you rely only on your own assets. If you need a business loan, the collateral for that loan will be your own personal assets. As a sole proprietor you are personally liable in the event of a lawsuit. Consider the possibility of obtaining professional liability insurance to protect your personal assets.

Red Alert

You must work with an accountant who has experience working with small business owners, especially sole proprietors. Ask other small business owners for recommendations. Your local Chamber of Commerce is also a good resource when looking for an accountant.

Success Strategy

Consider taking out a personal disability policy to protect you and your family in case you are no longer able to work.

As a sole proprietor you don't have an easily accessible support network. You can't just walk down the hall and ask a colleague for help, an opinion, or advice. It can be quite a lonely life at times. Sole proprietors have a significant need for a solid support network of professional colleagues upon whom they can rely. Set aside some time each month to network and keep in touch with these people even if you don't have a particular question or dilemma to resolve. And always be ready to help others in your network. You don't want to get a reputation as someone who is always looking for help but never offers any.

PARTNERSHIP

In a partnership each partner is committed to providing specific skills and expertise to the business and to sharing the expenses and risks. The skills and expertise are provided for an agreed upon share of the business's profits.

There are two types of partnerships: general partnerships and limited partnerships. In a general partnership, two or more people start a business. They agree on how business is conducted and how profits, risks, debts, and liabilities are shared among them. Note that profits, risks, etc., don't have to be divided equally among partners. Different agreements may mean different percentages.

In a limited partnership the partnership is registered and a franchise fee (a fee charged by the state to file a certificate of limited partnership) must be paid. Under limited partnership one or more limited partners invests in the business, though they are not involved in daily operations. General partners, who are responsible for all business debts, handle daily management. The limited partners are liable only for the amount of money they have invested in the business.

• *Success Strategy* •

Unless you can count on many limited partner investors, limited partnerships are not a good choice for a new business venture because of the complex paperwork and numerous legal filings. A general partnership is much easier to establish and maintain.

Here are a few essential points to remember about partnerships:

- *Never* enter into a partnership unless you have a written agreement or contract that has been reviewed by an attorney with expertise in partnership agreements. Be absolutely sure that you understand your risks, what you are expected to contribute in terms of money as well as in skills and knowledge, what share of the profits are yours, your liabilities, and your responsibility for debts.
- Sometimes additional partners are recruited simply because the business needs additional financing. If you need money rather than additional skills

or expertise, consider looking for an investor or limited partner. Do not recruit additional general partners whose only contribution is money.

- Successful partnerships depend in part on each partner contributing a unique set of perspectives and talents. You may be attracted to partners who have the same outlook, skills, and interests that you have. It's a better idea to find partners who can bring a variety of skills and viewpoints to the business. If all of the partners have similar expertise (and weaknesses) you run the risk of compounding your weaknesses and limiting your abilities.

- Make sure that you hire an attorney with experience in partnerships to establish a contract that covers important contingencies such as:
  - What happens if one of the partners becomes disabled or dies?
  - Is a buy-out agreement part of the contract?
  - If one or more partners decide to leave the partnership, must their shares of the business be offered to the remaining partners before they are offered to anyone else?

- Some entrepreneurs recommend that an automatic partnership dissolution date be inserted into the original letter of agreement or contract. This allows all involved partners to review the partnership and renegotiate based on company performance and the success of the interpersonal aspects of the partnership. The date is set in advance, and partners do not need to worry about the possibility of offending each other if one or more of them wants to review the partnership agreement.

There are a number of advantages to forming a partnership. It is generally easier to obtain financing since partners typically have more assets than sole proprietors. Additionally, the risks of the business are dispersed among one or more individuals. If one partner dies or becomes disabled the business goes on, providing this is part of the partnership contract. The remaining partners can keep the business going and, if necessary, secure new partners.

Partnerships bring a variety of skills, expertise, and perspectives to a business rather than the talents of just one person. Partnerships provide emotional support and camaraderie. Partners are people with whom to discuss ideas, talk over problems, and share stories.

There are also disadvantages to partnerships. It is doubtful that partners will always agree about all aspects of the business. As a result, disagreements and quarrels may occur between partners. If there are more disagreements than agreements the business will probably fail. Even if it does not fail outright, the work environment under such circumstances would be very unpleasant.

As a partner, you are legally liable for the actions of the other partners. You are accountable to your partners and they are accountable to you. Partners need to check with each other prior to arranging time off, leaving work early, purchasing equipment, hiring employees, etc. For people who dislike sharing control, partnerships can be unendurable.

CHOOSING A PARTNER

Choosing a partner is almost like choosing a spouse. You need to be there for each other in good times and in bad. You need to be able to disagree and to resolve disagreements. Successful partnerships depend on all of the partners' abilities to work together productively. Here are some issues to consider when choosing a partner.

- **Choosing a family member as a partner:** Think twice before making a family member a partner. Families have disintegrated over problems that evolve in a partnership. That doesn't mean that family partnerships can't or won't work. It just means that it can be extremely difficult to separate business life from family life.

- **Choosing a close friend as a partner:** Partnering with a close friend has the same risks as partnering with a family member. Friendships have dissolved over business deals. Additionally you may want to go into partnership with a friend simply because you have similar interests and skills. Your talents should complement but not duplicate each other's.

- **Choosing a colleague as a partner:** The ideal partnership is one in which two or more people who respect and admire each other's professional skills, knowledge, and expertise enter into a contractual business arrangement. It may not seem as comfortable as going into business with someone who is close to you (e.g., family or friends) but it will probably be easier to maintain a business rapport with a colleague. Regardless of your choice, you need to come to agreements about hours, time off, division of labor and profits, hiring and firing practices, client selection, ethics, what happens in the event one partner dies or becomes disabled, etc. All aspects of partnership must be part of a written contract even if (or especially if) partnering with family members or close friends.

LIMITED LIABILITY COMPANY

The limited liability company (LLC) is a relatively new type of business structure. It is treated as a partnership for American income tax purposes, and it costs less to form and maintain than a corporation. An LLC's owners are referred to as principals and are granted protection from personal liability like a corporation. However, an LLC dissolves whenever an owner dies and costs more to set up and maintain than a sole proprietorship.

• Success Strategy •••••••••••••••

LCC regulations vary from state to state. Investigate your own state's regulations carefully.

CORPORATIONS

Corporations, the most complex form of business legal structure, are legal organizations that exist separately from their owners. Because of this separation the personal liability of the owners is limited, but a double taxation on earnings (corporate tax and personal tax) puts this type of business at a tax disadvantage. A corporation has the term *Inc.* or *Corp.* after its name.

There are a number of advantages to being incorporated. This type of business structure projects an impressive business image and legally survives its owners. The personal liability of its owners and stockholders is limited. Raising capital is easier than with other types of business legal structures because corporations can sell stocks and bonds. Corporations are generally easier to sell because they exist separately from their owners. However, a majority of voting stockholders must agree to any sale.

There are, of course, disadvantages to being incorporated. Corporations involve extensive, on-going paperwork and record keeping and are usually expensive to start and maintain.

Small business owners may choose the S corporation as an option preferable to a regular (also known as C) corporation. In an S corporation, both income and losses are passed to shareholders and included in their individual tax returns, so there is only one level of federal tax to pay.

S corporations must file articles of incorporation, hold shareholder and director meetings, maintain meeting minutes, and allow shareholders voting rights concerning major decisions. Note that the costs of establishing an S corporation are similar to those of a C corporation.

CONCLUSION

Selecting a business structure should be done with great care and consideration. Assistance from a qualified accountant is essential, and legal counsel is often advisable. Prior to choosing your business structure, familiarize yourself with the advantages and disadvantages of each and select the one which best meets the needs of your business. The following table provides an overview of important aspects of each business structure.

Figure 3: Overview of Business Structures

Structure	Advantages	Disadvantages
Sole Proprietorship	Owner has complete control. Owner is independent and autonomous. Owner keeps all profits. Owner is not burdened with excessive paperwork and tax issues.	Owner can rely only on his/her own assets. Owner is personally liable in the event of a lawsuit. Owner does not have an easily accessible support network.
Partnership	Risks are shared. Variety of skills and expertise are shared. Financing is more easily obtained.	Disagreements occur. Control is shared. Partners are legally liable for each other's actions.
Limited Liability Company (LLC)	Principals face only limited liability. Treated as a partnership for tax purposes. Costs less to form and maintain than a corporation.	Dissolves whenever an owner dies. Costs more to form and maintain than a sole proprietorship.

Continued

Structure	Advantages	Disadvantages
Corporation	Exists separately from its owners.	Has a double taxation on earnings.
	Personal liability is limited.	Requires extensive paperwork and record keeping.
	Capital is more easily raised.	Expensive to start and maintain.

RESOURCES

Drake, S. M., (2001). *Freelancing for Dummies.* New York: Hungry Minds, Inc.

Lesonsky, R. (2004). *Start Your Own Business (3rd ed.).* Canada: Entrepreneur Press.

Shenson, H., & Nicholas, T. (1993). *The Complete Guide to Consulting Success.* Dearborn: Dearborn Publishing Group.

Sortino, J., & Shelly, S. (1999). *The Complete Idiot's Guide to Being a Successful Entrepreneur.* New York: Alpha Books.

SEVEN

Protecting Yourself and Your Business

It is essential that you protect yourself and the products and services your business provides. One way to protect yourself is to fully comprehend the relevant components of any contract or written agreement. Another is to recognize and initiate necessary actions to protect your intellectual property.

CONTRACTS AND LETTERS OF AGREEMENT

What is the difference between a contract and a letter of agreement? A letter of agreement is a legally enforceable document that confirms that the parties involved have agreed to a working relationship. This relationship is generally in the form of providing specific goods or services to a designated client. A contract is also a legally enforceable document confirming a working relationship. A contract, however, outlines in specific detail the terms agreed upon by the parties involved in the working relationship. Most companies and entrepreneurs prefer the use of a simple contract.

Here are some items that should be part of every contract:
- the names of all parties involved
- the date the contract becomes effective and the date it concludes (if applicable)
- a clear description of the product or services to be provided to the client

- a definite date for delivering agreed upon products and services or project completion
- how much and when you will be paid, including whether or not you will be paid for expenses (e.g., phone calls, travel, copying materials, etc.)
- the consequences for failure to pay you on time
- what to do if either party involved wants to terminate the contract prior to the delivery of products and services or project completion
- signatures of the parties involved and the date of signatures

Red Alert

Read all letters of agreement and contracts very carefully before you sign them. Do not sign unless all of your questions and concerns have been addressed to your satisfaction.

INTELLECTUAL PROPERTY

Intellectual property is the heart and soul of your business. Intellectual property refers to the ideas that you translate into products and services and which can, for a limited amount of time, be protected by a patent, trademark, and/or copyright.

PATENT

A patent is a proprietary right—the right to exclude other persons, companies, organizations, etc., from making, using, or selling your invention. The United States (U.S.) government grants a patent for a period of 20 years from the date on which the patent application is filed. At the end of 20 years, the patent becomes part of the public domain and anyone may make, sell, or use it.

The U. S. Patent and Trademark Office (PTO) (**www.uspto.gov**) is responsible for reviewing patent applications. The application process is complex and it is advisable to obtain the services of a patent attorney or patent agent to prepare your application. The PTO does not assist inventors to complete their applications. In addition to the complexity of the application, you must be prepared to pay a least $4,000 in application and maintenance fees.

Your invention must meet a number of criteria before the PTO will consider granting it a patent. These include the following:

Red Alert

In the United States, the first person, organization, etc., to invent something has the first right to file for a patent. However, in other countries, the first to file has the first right. United States patents are effective only within the United States, its territories, and its possessions.

- Inventions must be classifiable as one of the following: process (industrial or technical), machine, manufactured article, chemical compositions, or new and useful improvement of any of the other classifications.
- The invention must be new. It cannot be known or used by others or described in any publication anywhere in the world prior to applying for a patent.
- The invention must be significantly different from what already exists. In other words you cannot patent an invention that simply changes the size of someone else's invention.
- The invention must be useful.

TRADEMARK

A trademark is a word(s), symbol, or design that identifies a particular product or business. For example, the golden arches located outside a fast food restaurant immediately identify it as a McDonald's. If you own a trademark you have the right to stop others from using the same or similar mark. However, it does not give you the right to prevent others from making or selling the same products and services—only a patent can do that. You claim trademark rights by using the mark or filing an application to federally register the mark with the PTO.

• *Success Strategy* • • • • • • • • • • • • • • •
You do not need to apply to the PTO prior to using the mark. However, federal registration of the mark identifies you as its owner.

Trademarks can last indefinitely, as long as you use the trademark. An actual term of use is 10 years, but you can renew the registration as many times as you want to.

COPYRIGHT

Copyrights protect original works of writers, composers, screenwriters, and computer programmers, both published and unpublished, in all types of media, including the Internet. Note that a copyright does not protect an idea but how that idea is expressed. The Copyright Act gives the owner of copyrighted materials the exclusive right to publish, distribute, perform, or display the materials publicly. Copyrights registered by the Copyright Office of the Library of Congress (**www.copyright.gov**) generally last for the lifetime of the copyright holder plus 70 years. After that time it goes into the public domain. Copyright is documented by writing the word copyright (copyright 2005 Allison Gannon) or with the copyright symbol (© 2005 Allison Gannon).

You do not need to register your original work with the Copyright Office to obtain protection under the law. However, consider the following advantages to obtaining a copyright:
- Registering your copyright establishes a public record of the copyright.
- You can not file an infringement lawsuit unless your copyright is registered.
- Registering within three months after your work is published or before someone infringes on your work allows you to claim statutory damages and attorney's fees in a legal court of law.

Your business name is also something you want to protect. The following section will help you to choose an appropriate name for your new business.

CHOOSING A BUSINESS NAME

Choosing the name of your business is one of the most important decisions you'll make as an entrepreneur. The right name can help generate business and attract clients. The wrong name can discourage clients.

Here are some suggestions for naming your business:

- You may wish to choose a business name that describes, or at least refers to, your products and services.
- Consider using your own name as part of your business name. This is especially helpful if you have a good reputation in your chosen field.
- Avoid selecting a name that contains over-used phrases or words, is politically incorrect, or is confusing.

You may want to combine a logo as part of your business name and use it on your business cards. It should complement the image you want to project. Choose a professional name and logo. Do not select an overly "cute" name such as "Nurturing Nurses" if you want to stimulate serious business interest. A flowered business card may be fine for a decorating business or an elegant tearoom but not for a management consultant. When people see your business card or hear your business name they should immediately realize that they are dealing with a highly competent professional. Remember that your business name and advertisements (e.g., business cards, stationery, brochures) must reflect you and the image you want to foster.

You do not need to spend a great deal of money on professional looking business cards and stationery. Major office supply stores print significant quantities of these materials at very little cost. They have a variety of styles, colors, graphics, and fonts to choose from and produce professional-looking products at low cost.

> ### • *Success Strategy* • • • • • • • • • • • • •
>
> Carry a supply of business cards with you at all times. Successful entrepreneurs have made contact with potential clients at professional conferences as well as soccer games, the theater, and church picnics. Never miss an opportunity to network!

You'll want to be sure that your name is not already in use by another business. Do not infringe on a legally protected name, because you may be made to relinquish the name and lose the money you spent on marketing a name that you must stop using. *Home-Based Businesses for Dummies* offers some excellent tips to determine whether your business name is already in use. These include the following:

- Check telephone books and government offices. Check trade directories, local courthouses, county recorders, and the Federal Trademark Register.
- Do an Internet search. Type your potential business name into your search engine. Check the Internet Yellow Pages at **www.switchboard.com** and **www.infospace.com**.
- Perform a trademark search using databases such as the U. S. Patent and Trademark Office.

RESOURCES

Allen, K. (2001). *Entrepreneurship for Dummies.* New York: Wiley Publishing.

Drake, S. M. (2001). *Freelancing for Dummies.* New York: Hungry Minds, Inc.

Edwards, P., Edwards, S., & Economy, P. (2000). *Home-Based Business for Dummies.* Foster City: CA: IDG Books.

EIGHT

Zoning and Licensing Issues

Zoning and licensing regulations affect your business regardless of whether it is located in an office building or in your own home. If you violate any of these regulations and laws, no matter how innocently, you will be held accountable.

ZONING REGULATIONS

All forms of government that have jurisdiction over your business location, whether they are local, state, or federal, have rules and regulations about how you can or cannot run your business. If you violate any of these rules and regulations you run the risk of being fined or even of having your business closed. Zoning laws are primarily designed to keep residential and business areas apart.

Some laws are specific to the type of business you conduct. For example, if you want to open a business selling nursing uniforms, equipment, and novelties in a residential area the resulting traffic, deliveries, and advertisements (e.g., signs advertising your business) would disrupt the area and probably arouse the wrath of your neighbors as well. Establishing such a business would be prohibited by local zoning laws. However, if you plan on starting a business that does not affect your neighborhood (e.g., freelance medical writer) you may be allowed to operate your business from within your home assuming that your business does not affect traffic patterns or the visual or environmental aspects of the residential area.

There are a number of zoning issues that can and will affect your business. These include the following:

- parking restrictions
- traffic limitations
- advertising signage
- hours, types, and frequency of deliveries
- the use of dangerous and hazardous materials
- the number of people employed by your business and the types of jobs that they perform
- noise, smoke, and odor that may be generated by your business
- the percentage of your home (if you operate a home-based business) that is devoted to business endeavors

Suppose you live in an area that is zoned as residential, but you really want to operate a home-based business. You have two options:

- Request a variance. In some locations, you may only need to complete some relatively brief paperwork. However, in other locations you may need to have a public hearing in front of your city council or zoning board. Call or visit your zoning board for detailed instructions.
- Take action to change the rules and regulations that prevent you from opening your business. This could take considerable time and money. You

may even need to lobby for a change in legislation or file a lawsuit. Weigh the advantages and disadvantages of taking such action against finding another location for your business.

Success Strategy

Consider seeking legal counsel before taking any definite action.

SCENARIO ANALYSIS

The following scenarios deal with zoning issues that are not uncommon with home-based businesses.

Anna designs and sells nursing products (uniforms, gifts, novelties, equipment) advertised in a catalog and on her Web site. She runs her business from home. Although no customers or vendors related to the business come to Anna's home, she receives fairly frequent deliveries via UPS, but no more than some of her neighbors do. Anna lives in a zoned residential area but has never had any problems obtaining a business license nor have her neighbors ever complained about Anna's business activities. In fact, most of the people living in Anna's residential development are not even aware that Anna runs a home-based business.

Recently a new neighbor, Jackie, moves into the development, two houses away from Anna's home. Jackie asks Anna what she does for a living. When Jackie hears about the home-based business she decides to start a petition among the other residents of the neighborhood in an attempt to stop Anna's business activities. Anna tries to talk to Jackie but Jackie refuses to discuss her concerns, stating only that they live in a residential area not a business district. Jackie also says she is afraid that property values will decrease because of Anna's business.

What can Anna do to alleviate this problem?

- Assess the validity of Jackie's concerns about property values. Check with real estate agents as well as the local zoning board.
- Find out if Jackie has concerns in addition to the property value issue. Has she had problems with neighbors who operated home-based businesses in the past? Have other types of problems surfaced between Anna's family and Jackie's family? (e.g., their respective children don't get along).
- Determine how much support Jackie has among the other neighbors. Attempt to solicit support for the home-based business among sympathetic neighbors.
- Consult with zoning and licensing officials. Since Anna has obtained a business license without difficulty there must be a precedent for home-based businesses in Anna's neighborhood.

Jackie presents her concerns and the petition to local officials. Anna must now appear before these officials at a formal hearing. The meeting is open to Jackie and other residents of the neighborhood. What should Anna do to prepare for this hearing?

- She should obtain the services of an attorney experienced in zoning issues and small business practices.
- She can ask neighbors sympathetic to her cause to attend the meeting on her behalf.
- She should, by all means, stay calm and objective and not give in to anger.
- She should gather objective data to show that the business does not disrupt neighborhood activities, damage property, or endanger residents. She can also document how many business-related deliveries are received weekly and compare this to deliveries received by others in the neighborhood.

At the hearing, Anna requests a variance to run her home-based business in a residential neighborhood. She must now appear at a public hearing in front of the city council and zoning board. How should she prepare for this hearing?

- Again, Anna must be familiar with zoning regulations governing her neighborhood. She also needs to obtain appropriate legal assistance.
- Anna must complete all necessary paperwork requested by public officials and submit it in a timely manner.
- She should ask the public officials what types of questions she will be asked during the hearing. She should prepare her responses carefully and put them in writing (with the help of her attorney).

Success Strategy

Most people who appear in front of public officials become a bit nervous. If you are required to appear at such a meeting you don't want to seem unsure of yourself or forget any important points. Statements should not be read verbatim, but used as a resource. Practice responding to all types of questions, including those that are argumentative.

- Anna should talk to other business owners who have had to deal with similar meetings. They will be able to supply helpful tips on how to cope with this type of challenge.
- Above all, Anna must be prepared to discuss her business endeavors and the measures she has taken to ensure that it will not disrupt her neighborhood.

LICENSING ISSUES

You always need a license to operate a business, including home-based businesses. The particulars depend on your local government. Talk to your local officials, describe your business, and ask for the necessary paperwork as well as instructions on completing it. Ask for any resources that might be available for small business owners.

• Success Strategy •••••••••••••

Your accountant will be able to help you to complete licensing paperwork.

A business license is the standard permit needed to operate your business locally. A home-based business may also require a home occupation permit. If you plan to sell products you will need a seller's permit. Tax issues concerning what products are taxable vary among states.

A state occupational license is required for persons practicing some occupations including nurses, physicians, daycare operators, and lawyers. Consult with your state licensing boards about obtaining appropriate licensure.

There may be additional regulations, such as Occupational Safety and Health Act (OSHA) regulations that impact your business. Just because you are unaware of some laws or regulations won't prevent you from being fined if you violate them. Your local Chamber of Commerce is an excellent resource for issues such as these.

CONCLUSION

Zoning and licensing laws vary among states and cities. Obtain necessary legal and financial counsel as you pursue your business interests. Home-based businesses may, in some cases, be operated from a residentially zoned neighborhood. To pursue this type of activity you need to obtain not only legal assistance, but the guidance of your local and state authorities. Make sure that your business endeavors adhere to all appropriate zoning and licensing regulations.

RESOURCES

Edwards, P., Edwards, S., & Economy, P. (2000). *Home-Based Business for Dummies.* Foster City, CA: IDG Books.

Hingston, P., & Alastari Balfour. (2001). *Working from Home.* New York: Dorling Kindersley.

Lesonsky, R. (2004). *Start Your Own Business (3rd ed.).* Canada: Entrepreneur Press.

Shenson, H., & Nicholas, T. (1993), *The Complete Guide to Consulting Success.* Dearborn: Dearborn Publishing Group.

Sortino, J., & Shelly, S. (1999). *The Complete Idiot's Guide to Being a Successful Entrepreneur.* New York: Alpha Books.

Unit Three

FINANCES

NINE

Developing a Business Plan

Many small business owners, especially sole proprietors, are surprised to hear that they need a business plan. A business plan is necessary to chart the direction of your business. A well-written business plan helps you to think logically and realistically about your business and reduces your chance of failure. A business plan also helps you measure how well you are achieving your goals and objectives. While you may have always thought of a business plan as merely something you must write in order to get funding or to help ensure that your business gets off to a good start, a business plan is a valuable tool for the entire span of your venture.

PURPOSE OF THE BUSINESS PLAN

A business plan makes you think about (and put in writing) the details of operating your business. Sometimes just putting things in writing helps you to recognize new opportunities for your business that you didn't think of before. Putting things in writing may also help you to identify problems that you never thought of. A business plan describes all aspects of your business so that you (and anyone else who reads it) can have a complete understanding of how your business functions. A sound business plan will be a big help when you discuss your business with people such as bankers, investors, potential partners, employees, and vendors.

Your business plan shows bankers as well as potential and actual investors how much capital is required to start and run your business and how it will be spent. The plan also helps demonstrate how you plan to generate income and repay loans as well as identify contingencies for responding to unanticipated business reversals or downturns in the economy.

Remember that a business plan is only worth something if you use it. A beautifully written and packaged plan that simply occupies computer space or sits on a shelf from one year to the next is useless. The plan must help you to determine where you are going, how you plan to get there, and how well you're achieving your goals and objectives.

COMPONENTS OF A BUSINESS PLAN

Executive Summary

The executive summary is the first section of your business plan, and is the most important part of your plan. It is a one or two page overview that describes the essential elements of your entire plan. While the executive summary is a logical lead for the reader of the plan, it is full of information you will not be completely clear on until you have finished writing your business plan. As a result, though the executive summary is the first section of your plan, it should be written last.

The executive summary is your entire business plan in miniature. It is often the only part of the plan that investors, bankers, potential partners, and some others will read. Busy people may scan the plan in its entirety but will carefully read the executive summary. The executive summary must grab the reader's attention with its first sentence by identifying the purpose of your business and its overall goals. You've got to make the reader want to know more about you and your business. Here are some examples:

- Mason's Performance Coaching is the tri-state leader in executive level management consulting services.
- Effective Education, Inc., designs and delivers continuing education guaranteed to improve job performance.
- Healthcare Graphics, Inc., guarantees the best in graphics design for health care systems and corporations.

If you've been in operation for any length of time you can briefly describe, using objective data, how you have achieved some of your goals. If yours is a new venture, describe how you intend to achieve your goals and why your business is going to be a success.

Tim Berry, in his excellent book, *Hurdle: The Book on Business Planning,* recommends that your write summaries of each of the other sections of your business plan (or opening paragraphs for each section) well enough so that you can compile them into an effective executive summary.

• Success Strategy

Write clear, concise summary paragraphs of each section of your business plan. Compile them as an executive summary and remember, the executive summary may be your one and only chance to impress those who receive your business plan.

Business Description

The next component of your business plan is the business description. This section includes critical comments about the nature of your business and an overview of the products and services it provides. Tell the reader what makes your business unique. Identify the purpose of your business and your over-all goal as a business owner. Place your mission, vision, and values statements here. These statements proclaim the social and personal values that will dictate how you conduct business. In fact, these statements make up the majority of this section of the business plan.

Your values statement is a clear, concise identification of the standards that guides your business through its day-to-day operations, its plans for the future, and the challenging decisions all business owners face.

For example, suppose you own and operate an online education business geared to meeting the continuing education needs of registered nurses. Your vision may include statements such as the following:

The Online Nursing Education Company exists to offer registered nurses online education programs that enhance their ability to provide high-quality patient care. Employees of the Online Nursing Education Company believe that:

- Learning is a life-long endeavor.
- Adults are self-directed learners who bring a background of rich life experiences to leaning activities.
- Nurses are responsible for identifying their educational needs, achieving their educational goals, and obtaining relevant educational experiences.
- Nurses have the right to expect that Online Nursing Education Company provides accredited, relevant, accurate information designed to help nurses improve their job performance.

The preceding vision statement gives the reader a great deal of information. It states the core beliefs of the individuals involved in the company and it shows that the purpose of this company is to fulfill these beliefs.

The vision of your business is the ideal image of what you want it to become. A good business vision is realistic, attainable, driven by values, inspirational, and future-oriented. For example, the Online Education Company's vision might be something like this:

> *It is the vision of the Online Education Company*
> *to be a leader in the provision of online continuing*

*nursing education throughout the United States
and Canada.*

The mission of a business is to express the purpose of your business to you, your employees, and even to individuals who are not officially part of your business. The mission statement must encompass your vision and values.

*It is the mission of the Online Education Company
to enhance the practice of nursing by providing
continuing education programs designed to increase
knowledge, skills, and professionalism.*

Your organizational structure should also be identified in the business description section. A complex business that employ a significant number of individuals may require that the organizational structure be a separate component of the business plan. However, most new entrepreneurs operate as sole proprietors or with a single partner and do not need a complex organizational structure. The purpose of including the organizational structure is to clarify who is involved in the development and distribution of your products and services.

Description of Products and Services

This section gives you the chance to describe in detail the products and services you provide, and to whom you provide them. It should be as detailed as necessary to give the reader a clear understanding of what it is you offer. The reader should know exactly what you provide, how you deliver your products and services, and how you plan to keep up with the demand for your products and services.

Include how much it costs to produce and sell your products and services, who uses them, and why. This section is written in terms of customer needs, benefits, and satisfaction. For example, the Online Education Company's description would include a rationale for providing Web-based education and why nurses benefit from the specific education programs their company offers.

The description of products and services also addresses how your products compare to those of your competitors. It is an opportunity to explain why customers should do business with you instead.

As you write this section you may discover new needs, identify new products and services, or discover a group of potential new customers. You may also discover that some of your plans are impractical. Writing a business plan provides you with a chance to objectively review what you plan to do and how and why you plan to do it.

Marketing

The marketing section of your business plan must convince readers that your business has the potential to significantly influence the consumers in your identified market to purchase your products and services. It identifies your current and targeted customers, the scope of your customer population, and your competition.

In this section, discuss how you analyze, plan, implement, and control those strategies designed to bring your products and services to the attention of your customers for the purpose of achieving the goals and objectives of your business. Describe your market, your customers, and your competition. Describe in detail how you plan to market your services.

Action Plan

The action plan identifies specific, measurable goals and objectives and action steps you intend to take to achieve each objective. These objectives must be realistic and achievable and they must include target completion dates. You must also identify who is responsible for carrying out the action steps. In essence, the action plan describes what you want to achieve, how you intend to achieve it, and within what time frame you plan to achieve it.

Finances

The financial section of your business plan describes your current financial status and what you expect it to be in the future. Document your expenses and income, cash-flow, and projected profit and loss.

GENERAL RECOMMENDATIONS

Under normal circumstances, a good business plan should be between 15 and 20 pages long. A longer plan may discourage people from reading and understanding it. (*You* might even lose interest in it.) A shorter plan will probably not contain all of the information that is essential for business success.

Success Strategy

Make two back-up CDs or discs of all of your indispensable documents.

Make sure that you make a back-up CD or disk of you plan. You don't want to lose it in the event of a computer crash, theft, or malfunction. Consider making two back-up CDs or disks and keep one of them in a location other than your office.

Your business plan is a "work in progress." It will reflect the impact that economics, societal pressures, and the demand for your products and services have on your business. You can review and rewrite components as these factors mandate. However, if you have a well-written plan, the format and major components remain consistent.

Review your plan at least annually. The areas that most often need updating and/or revision are the financial plan (annual budget) and the action plan, as goals and objectives evolve.

EVALUATING YOUR BUSINESS PLAN

Ask a trusted entrepreneurial colleague to review your business plan. Do not ask a close friend to review it because he or she may be hesitant to offer criticism. You are looking for someone with

Red Alert

Do not ask a direct competitor to review your plan!

solid business experience who isn't afraid to tell you the truth about what you're doing right—and wrong.

You should also review your plan for yourself. Ask yourself the following questions:

- Have I linked my goals and objectives to my mission, vision, and values?
- Does my business plan address ability to cope with change?
- Is the plan clear and concise? Is it easy to read? Is it up-to-date?
- Have I identified major opportunities?
- Have I identified strengths and weaknesses?
- Have I clearly identified my customers? Do I know what they purchase from me and why?
- Have I identified my competitors? Do I know how they do business? Have I lost any customers to them? Why or why not?
- Do my financial statements indicate that my business is on track? Why or why not?

You also need to understand the most common mistakes made when formulating a business plan. Avoid the following:

- **Failure to plan.** The most common mistake small business owners make is failing to plan and/or failing to put a plan in writing. There is no substitute for a well-written business plan. It is your road map. It tells you where you've gone, where you're going, and what changes you need to make along the way.
- **Failure to incorporate your personal values into your business plan.** If you ignore your mission, vision, and values, you'll lack direction. These statements reflect who you are as an individual and a business owner and will guide you in your business pursuits. Make sure that all of your business decisions are aligned with your guiding principles.

- **Failure to know and respect your clients.**
  Remember that the client always come first! Your
  existence depends upon your ability to meet their
  needs by providing excellent products and services.
  But make sure that you know how your clients
  define excellence. It may be different from your
  definition!
- **Failure to know and understand your
  competitors.** It's as important to know your
  competitors as it is to know your clients.
- **Failure to recognize your strengths and
  weaknesses.** Be proud of your strengths and work
  to improve your weaknesses.
- **Failure to compile a thorough business plan.**
  Some people assume that their budgets are their
  business plans. The budget is certainly a critical
  component of the plan but it is not the only
  component.

CONCLUSION

Your business plan is your guide to business implementation.
All entrepreneurs need to write concise, clear, user-friendly
business plans. The following table is an overview of the essential components of any business plan. Use it to write a plan that
works for you!

Figure 4: Business Plan Overview

Component	Description
Executive Summary	Most important part of the plan. Is the entire business plan in miniature. Composed of well-written summaries from each of the other sections of your business plan.
Business Description	Includes mission, vision, and values statements. Identifies the business's purpose and overall goals. Organizational structure is generally part of the business description in small businesses.
Description of Products and Services	Describes products and services in detail. Describes the costs involved in producing and delivering your services. Compares your services to the competition. Written in terms of customer needs, benefits, and satisfaction.
Marketing	Identifies your current and targeted customers, the scope of your customer population, and your competition. Describes your market, your customers, and your competition. Describes how you market your services.
Action Plan	Describes what you want to achieve, how you intend to achieve it, and within what time frame you plan to achieve it.
Finances	Describes your current financial status and what you expect it to be in the future.

RESOURCES

Allen, K. (2001). *Entrepreneurship for Dummies.* New York: Wiley Publishing.

Avillion, A. E. (2003). *Writing a Staff Development Plan: Business Strategies for the 21ˢᵗ Century.* Pensacola, FL: National Nursing Staff Development Organization.

Avillion, A. E. (2004). *A Practical Guide to Staff Development: Tools and Techniques for Effective Education.* Marblehead, MASS: hcPro

Berry, T. (1999). *Hurdle: The Book on Business Planning.* Eugene, OR: Palo Alto Software, Inc.

Kaufman, K. (2000). *Finance in Brief: Six Key Concepts for Healthcare Leaders.* Chicago: Health Administration Press.

Tiffany, P., & Peterson, S. (1997). *Business Plans for Dummies.* Foster City, CA: IDG Books.

TEN

Pricing Strategies

Determining how much your products and services are worth is critical to your success. If you set your fees too high, clients will not be willing to pay them. If you set them too low, clients may question your value or you may go out of business because of insufficient income. The idea is to find a compromise between "too high" and "too low."

DETERMINING DESIRED ANNUAL INCOME

In figuring out how to price your products and services, first determine the amount of money you need to meet your expenses. Calculate your personal monthly expenses. Do you have a monthly mortgage or rent payment? Do you make monthly health insurance payments? What is the average amount of money you spend on utilities on a monthly basis? Calculate your average monthly grocery bills, credit card payments, transportation, and any other expenses that occur on a monthly basis. The sum of all of these bills constitutes your monthly personal expenses.

Now, think about your business expenses. "Overhead" consists of all of your business's non-direct costs and non-salary expenses. These are expenses that exist even if you are not directly providing products and services. Such expenses include things like computers, fax machines, office furniture, Internet

services, telephone lines, licenses, office rent, repairs, maintenance, and office supplies. Since overhead doesn't directly
produce income, do what you can to keep these costs to a minimum.

Direct costs are the expenses required to create and deliver
your products and services. These include items such as travel
expenses, telephone calls, supplies, time spent in meetings with
clients, time spent preparing projects, etc. If you have employees, you need to determine what
they cost you monthly in terms
of salary and benefits.

Red Alert

Don't forget to include
estimated costs for
vacations and other non-
business activities.

After reviewing your
monthly business and personal
expenses, identify a target
figure for your desired yearly
income. Divide this figure by
48 to calculate your weekly
income. Base your weekly
income using 48 weeks instead of 52
weeks because you need to allow 4 weeks for vacation, sick time,
and other absences from work. Divide that figure by 5 to calculate your desired daily income.

PRICING METHODS

There are a number of workable pricing methods, several of
which are listed below. Evaluate them and decide which ones
are best for you. Pricing methods vary depending on the type of
work you do and who your clients are. Most entrepreneurs use
several methods, each of which has advantages and disadvantages. Here are some common pricing methods:

- **Flat Fee or Project Rate:** Project rates are easier
to accurately determine after you have some
entrepreneurial experience. If you agree to a flat
fee and the project becomes more complicated
or takes longer than you anticipate, you may
lose money. Past experience with similar types of

projects helps you to calculate a flat fee per project. For example, if you are developing continuing education programs for a client, experience tells you the approximate length of time, effort, and cost it takes you to prepare and deliver such a program. After you have enough experience preparing these types of programs, you become comfortable setting a flat fee or fee per project.

- **Hourly Fee:** An hourly rate is often charged by consultants. If you are to be paid by the hour, however, you and your client need to determine what constitutes "work." In addition to time actually spent with clients you must determine what other services are charged as billable hours? Do you include time spent on telephone calls with clients? Do you include time spent doing research? Do you include travel time? These issues must be discussed with your client and included in your contract. You will need to document your work-related activities and present a record of your billable hours to your client.

- **Retainer:** A retainer is a fee a client pays you to secure your availability to complete a project. Clients pay retainers to assure that a certain amount of an entrepreneur's time is devoted to their needs.

- **Fixed Rate per Day:** One of the biggest problems with a fixed rate per day method is that you and your client must agree on the definitions of a "day." Is it 8 hours? Is it 24 hours? You and your client must clearly agree on the definition of a day.

- **Payment per Product:** Some nurse entrepreneurs offer specific products for sale such as books, novelty items, or uniforms. Prices are established based on how much it costs to produce, advertise, and deliver such items. You may want to consider a discount rate if a client orders a large supply of products at one time or is a customer who orders often.

- **Payment by the Word or Page:** Entrepreneurs who earn their living by writing sometimes charge by the word or page. For example, some online education companies estimate that 3,000-4,000 words equals one contract hour, and they make payments based on the probable number of contract hours. Paying by the number of pages is a bit trickier. What is a page? Is there a mandatory number of lines per page? What are the margin settings? What is the size and type of font? All of these factors influence the printed page. Do not agree to a "pay per page" schedule unless you and your client agree to an exact definition of what constitutes a page.

GUIDELINES FOR PRICING

There are no hard and fast rules for pricing, but there are some basic principles to follow. First, stop and think before you set a price or agree to a client's offer of payment. Never quote a price on the spot. Assess the project and carefully calculate your fee. Use your networking contacts and mentors to stay up-to-date on pricing strategies for your type of business. The longer you are in business, the more comfortable you will become setting your fees. Experience offers a good understanding of the time, effort, and costs involved in running your business.

Determine your lowest acceptable fee for products and services and do not go below it. Do not agree to work for less than you know a project or service is worth. If you do, you may acquire a great deal of business due to your low prices, but you won't be able to meet your expenses let alone make a profit.

Keep good records for every project you complete or product you deliver. List all tasks and the amount of time and resources it took to complete those tasks. Identify what went wrong and what went right. Compare the income each project generated to its expenses. Use these records to help you establish fees for future products and services.

As you determine your pricing strategies, keep in mind the role pricing plays in acquiring and retaining clients.

- **Focus first and foremost on client satisfaction.** In your pricing strategy, as in every other aspect of your business relationship, treat each client as though he or she is the most important client you have.
- **Do terrific work.** Make sure that whatever products and services you offer are of consistently worth what you're charging for them.
- **Provide something that your competitors can't or won't provide.** Make your value apparent so you stand out from the crowd. Use marketing statements such as "We never miss a deadline," or "We guarantee delivery within 48 hours."
- **Build long-term relationships with reliable clients.** Reliable clients pay you on time, give clear-cut descriptions of what they want and when they want it, and offer useful, constructive feedback.

Success Strategy

Learn to recognize unreliable clients. These are clients who fail to pay you on time, fail to honor terms of contracts or letters of agreement, and/or fail to give you clear direction. Don't work for these clients.

There are times when you need to increase your fees. There are also times when you may need to decrease your fees. Below are some circumstances that dictate each of these actions.

You need to increase your prices if:

- You have under-priced your products or services. This is probably the case if you are not earning enough to cover your expenses, if your prices are too far below your competitors' prices, and/or if you are failing to generate a profit.

- Your expenses have increased. If the costs of operating your business have increased you can increase your prices, decrease your operating expenses, or accept reduced profits.
- The marketplace dictates an increase. Changes in the economy and/or in the pricing strategies of your competitors may trigger a need for you to increase your fees.

You need to decrease your prices if:

- You have over-priced your products and services. This may generate a profit initially, but it may make you lose enough clients that your bottom line eventually suffers. You will never be indispensable to any client. There are always other entrepreneurs who would love to have your clients as their own.
- You want to reward regular customers. Offering long-term loyal clients a discount is a way of showing appreciation and enhancing loyalty.

Red Alert

Under-pricing is not the only reason for the preceding problems. You may have insufficient business or are taking too long to complete projects. Before you increase your prices, evaluate the amount of business you have and how long it takes you to deliver products and services.

FEE NEGOTIATION

Determine your bottom line, and never accept a fee that is unfair. You may need to accept the lowest acceptable fee for a project (especially if you are still building your reputation as an entrepreneur) but do not go below your bottom line. Do not start by quoting your lowest acceptable fee. Start with a figure that is fair but allows you a good profit. You often need to negotiate with your client about fees and expenses. But, as you negotiate, remember your bottom line and don't go below it.

Stay calm and be objective when negotiating. Be prepared to deal with and to suggest counter proposals, but don't violate your own minimum acceptable fee. For example, suppose you start by quoting a fee of $1,500 for a particular project. You're absolute minimum is $1,000. Your client offers $1,200. You counter with $1,350, an ultimately acceptable figure for both of you. However, don't be afraid to say, "No." There are times when you simply will not be able to afford to work for a client who is unable or unwilling to pay you what you are worth.

If you have been actively pursuing a new client and truly believe that he or she could become a long-term, valuable source of business, you may decide to work for less money than you would normally. If the client is pleased with your work and comes to rely on you, you may eventually be able to raise your fees without too much difficulty. However, this strategy is always risky. You need to decide if the risk is worth taking.

Now, what about the client who fails to pay you on time or doesn't pay you at all? First, always have a written contract or a written letter of agreement that documents how much and when you will be paid. Include a penalty for late fees in your agreement.

Red Alert

Remember, never quote a client a fee without thinking about it first. Give yourself a chance to review the job you are asked to do, the work involved, and what your services are worth. Set your fees accordingly!

Make sure you send an invoice for every job you complete and maintain a copy of every invoice you send. A sample invoice follows.

Figure 5: Sample Invoice

Andrea Nelson
CEO, Continuing Education Plus
601 Fairway Lane
Hazlewood, PA 12247

Invoice

Date: April 21, 2005

Invoice # 15: Madison Healthcare System

Fee due: $5,000

Date Due: May 15, 2005

Project: Computer Based Learning Arrhythmia Course

Tax ID# 177-20-1234

An invoice includes your company's name and address, the date the invoice is sent, an invoice number (in this case, this is the 15th invoice sent to Madison Healthcare System, a regular client), the fee, the date payment is due, and the project for which you are requesting payment. In the case of a sole proprietor, the tax ID# is your social security number.

With a contract or letter of agreement to support your claim, and a record of invoices in your files, you can pursue payment. Include a late fee penalty in your contracts and agreements. Here are some steps to take when clients fail to pay.

- Telephone your client personally. Stay calm and objective. Extend your client the courtesy of a conversation and give him or her the opportunity to explain why your fee is late. Call the client within 48 hours of failing to receive your payment on time. Most customers respond to telephone reminders and a direct conversation. E-mail reminders do not allow the personal conversation that seems to have more of an impact.
- After speaking to your client send out a formal past-due notice. If your contract guarantees that

the client pays a late fee penalty (e.g., 10% of the total fee for each week payment is delayed) make sure to include that in the past-due notice and identify the total amount now due to you.

- If you are working on a long-term project and agreed to be paid in increments, do not supply any additional products or services until payment is received.

- If you can't resolve the problem yourself and the fee is significant to your business survival, you may want to enlist the services of a collections agency or a mediator. A mediator is an objective third party whose job it is to help you and your client achieve a satisfactory solution. If this strategy fails, you can enlist the services of a collections agency. Be aware, however, that the expense involved in hiring mediators and collections agencies can be considerable.

- If all else fails you may consider taking your client to court. The extent to which you pursue your fee is up to you. Will it cost you more in time, money, and aggravation to go to court than it would to accept the loss and end the business relationship? The decision is yours.

CONCLUSION

Determining your pricing strategy is one of the most significant challenges you face as an entrepreneur. Here are some helpful Web resources that facilitate pricing research. These sites offer information about all types of businesses, their profits, losses, fees, and client base. It is an easy way to benchmark business practices and scope out the competition.

- Business Wire: **www.businesswire.com**
- Public Register's Annual Report Service: **www.prars.com**
- Hoover's Online: **www.hoovers.com**

- Small Business Administration: **www.sba.gov**
- Service Corps of Retired Executives (SCORE): **www.score.org**, a free online business advice group

RESOURCES

Allen, K. (2001). *Entrepreneurship for Dummies.* New York: Wiley Publishing

Avillion, A. E. (2003). *Writing a Staff Development Plan: Business Strategies for the 21ˢᵗ Century.* Pensacola, FL: National Nursing Staff Development Organization.

Drake, S. M. (2001). *Freelancing for Dummies.* New York: Hungry Minds.

Edwards, P., Edwards, S., & Economy, P. (2000). *Home-Based Business for Dummies.* Foster City, CA: IDG Books.

Hingston, P., & Balfour, A. (2001). *Working from Home.* New York: Dorling Kindersley.

Lewis, L. (1999). Pricing Strategies for Freelance Medical Writers. *American Medical Writers Association Journal,* 14(2), 18-21.

ELEVEN

Overview of Financial Issues

This chapter introduces basic financial and accounting concepts for the nurse entrepreneur. Remember that first and foremost you need an excellent accountant who has experience working with small business owners. However, even with the guidance of such an accountant, you still need to understand the basic components of your business's financial issues. As you start out, you may not be able to afford the services of a full-time accountant. Most entrepreneurial businesses are a one or two person endeavor. Therefore, one of the many hats you'll be wearing is that of accountant. You must also understand financial issues so that you can appropriately price your products and services to generate profit, determine your break-even point, and perform cost-benefit analyses. Nurse entrepreneurs must be knowledgeable about financial issues so that they can assess their companies' financial soundness.

CHOOSING AN ACCOUNTANT

To determine what accounting services you require, ask yourself the following questions:
- Will you be handling the day-to-day financial operations yourself? If so, what do you expect your accountant to do? Or will you need an accountant

to handle all of the financial aspects of your business (e.g., budget statements, payroll, etc.).
- Do you have enough business to put an accountant on retainer?
- Do you anticipate needing only minimal assistance, such as help with quarterly and annual tax preparation? (Note: You'll need to pay estimated local, state, and federal taxes on a quarterly basis.)

As you think about the preceding questions, consider also that a good accountant can assist you by:
- maintaining employee records
- preparing budget statements
- issuing invoices
- filing tax returns
- writing checks
- paying bills
- balancing checkbooks
- preparing financial statements
- issuing payroll

After you decide what it is you need from an accountant, you can find one in a number of ways. You can ask other small business entrepreneurs for recommendations. Financial advisors are another good resource for recommendations. Your local Chamber of Commerce will probably have a number of accountants as members and can also provide you with assistance.

Success Strategy

As a small business owner you will most likely receive better service from a small to medium sized accounting firm.

Interview a few accountants prior to making your selection. Don't choose an accountant based on a single recommendation; you need to be comfortable working with your accountant. A good accountant is:

- a Certified Public Accountant (CPA) (meaning that he or she has met minimum education requirements and passed an exam),
- a good listener,
- willing to take the time to listen to your concerns ,
- interested in understanding your business goals and objectives,
- able to help with tax planning and filing,
- accustomed to working with small business entrepreneurs, and
- willing to discuss what services he or she can offer a small business owner.

BASIC FINANCIAL TERMINOLOGY

The following terms are basic to understanding the financial aspects of your business.

Assets: Assets are items, both tangible and intangible, that are worth money. Examples of tangible assets include cash, land, buildings, and equipment. Intangible assets include patents and trademarks that protect your products and services.

Liabilities: Liabilities are monies that you (as a business owner) owe to others, such as bills, employees' salaries, mortgage or rent payments, or loan debts.

Owners Equity: Owners equity is the difference between the value of your assets and the amount of money you owe on your liabilities.

Income Statement: Also called the operating statement, revenue statement, or the profit and loss statement—the income statement shows net profit or net loss and is expressed mathematically as:

revenues – expenses = net profit or net loss

Your income statement tells you whether you are operating at a profit or a loss.

Revenue: Revenue is income generated as a result of selling your products and services.

Expense: Expense is the money you spend to conduct business.

Profit: Profit is the difference between revenue and expenses. Profit is represented by the equation: **revenue – expenses = profit.**

Cash Flow Statement: A record of cash input and output at the time they occur. It shows how much cash you have on hand, when you earn it, and when you spend it.

Balance Sheet: A balance sheets describes the value of your business at a specific point in time taking into account assets, liabilities, and owners' equity. For example, at the end of the year you calculate the value of all assets and all liabilities and subtract the two to determine your owner's equity.

Fixed Costs: Fixed costs are those that stay the same each month. For example, rent or the cost of Internet service is generally the same every month.

Variable Costs: Costs that change depending on use, economic conditions, etc. For example, suppose you design, manufacture, and sell nurses' uniforms and novelty items. The cost of the materials varies depending on how many you make each month and any changes in the cost of the materials (e.g., fabric) you must purchase to make your products.

Break-Even Point: The break-even point is reached when your total expenses equal your total revenue.

Cost-Benefit Analysis: Cost-benefit analysis is the comparison of the cost of an item or action to the value the item or action brings to your business.

As a nurse entrepreneur, you are most likely operating a relatively small business and do not need a complex method of budgeting and accounting (at least not yet). Sit down with your accountant and ask him or her to help you set up your budgeting and accounting system.

A relatively simple system will most likely work best. Here is an example of a very simple, yet workable, system.

- Maintain an "accounts due" file. Keep copies of all invoices. When the invoice is paid, staple the check stub to the invoice, date it, and move it to accounts paid file.

- Maintain a "business expense" file. When you spend money, keep a record of what you spent, why you spent it, and when you spent it.

- Keep an ongoing record of business expenses and income for tax purposes. There are numerous computer software programs available that help organize these records. If you keep it up to date and have accurate accounts due, accounts paid, and business expense files, you will find it easy to prepare your taxes every quarter.

CONCLUSION

A simple accounting system meets the needs of most nurse entrepreneurs. Choose a qualified accountant whom you trust and work together to develop your accounting and budgeting systems. Become familiar with basic financial terms and be prepared to analyze your business's balance sheets and income and cash-flow statements. You, not your accountant, are ultimately responsible for the financial health of your business.

Red Alert

If you are a sole proprietor consider granting check-writing authority to someone. If you are the only person who has the authority to write checks on your business account no one will be able to pay bills and handle business expenses in the even you become seriously ill or are injured. Your spouse, a trusted colleague, or adult children are examples of individuals to whom you could grant check-writing authority.

RESOURCES

Allen, K. (2001). *Entrepreneurship for Dummies.* New York: Wiley Publishing.

Berry, T. (1999). *Hurdle: The Book on Business Planning.* Eugene, OR: Palo Alto Software, Inc.

Drake, S. M. (2001). *Freelancing for Dummies.* New York: Hungry Minds.

Edwards, P., Edwards, S., & Economy, P. (2000). *Home-Based Business for Dummies.* Foster City, CA: IDG Books.

Unit Four

MARKETING YOUR BUSINESS

TWELVE

Client Satisfaction

In order to figure out how to satisfy your clients, first carefully consider who they are. Clients can be individuals or organizations. For example, if you are a consultant specializing in management development, your clients are the organizational leaders who hire you as well as the fledgling mangers who require your help in developing their managerial skills. You may also choose to think of the health care organization as a client, since your ability to help develop managers ultimately influences the effectiveness of the organization. Your relationship with your clients will be influenced, in part, by their demographic profiles and their personal and professional characteristics.

Demographics include what types of products and services clients purchase, how often and how much they purchase, and when they make their purchases. For example, a management consultant would want to know if clients require management development on an on-going basis, at certain times during the year, or only when problems surface.

Personal and professional characteristics include those factors that influence clients' beliefs and behaviors. Are they risk takers, conservative in purchasing decisions, eager to embrace change; are they traditionalists? If you, as a management development consultant, are known for facilitating change and promoting "cutting edge" management strategies, you would probably work well with clients who are risk takers and change advocates. An organization known for its autocratic management style, however, would not want to work with a consultant who advocates shared decision making. Thus, an important factor in your ability to satisfy your clients is the degree to which you and your potential clients are aligned in your values, beliefs, and modes of organizational functioning. This doesn't mean you need to absolutely agree about everything. It simply means that you must have certain basic philosophical and practical values and beliefs in common.

•• *Success Strategy* ••••••••••••••••

Some entrepreneurs use the words "client" and "customer" interchangeably. Historically, "client" refers to someone who purchases the professional services of another person, and it is the term generally preferred by most entrepreneurs. "Customer" is more likely to refer to someone who purchases manufactured products such as uniforms, novelty items, and equipment. There is no rigid rule about terminology, but "client" is generally the preferred term in current use.

CULTIVATING YOUR BEST CLIENTS

Who are your best clients? These are the clients who trust your judgment, are flexible, pay you promptly, continue to do business with you, and refer you to others. The following statements describe the ideal client:

- The client's basic business philosophy, vision, and values are aligned with mine.
- The client and I have similar beliefs about problem solving.
- The client and I have similar beliefs about management styles.
- The client and I are able to discuss projects in an honest, straightforward manner without becoming defensive or angry.

- The client and I evaluate the quality of my work and the progress being made on a regular basis.
- The client and I have compatible communication styles.
- The client adheres to the terms of our contract or letter of agreement.
- The client pays me on time.
- The client continues to ask for my services.
- The client recommends my services to others.

Success Strategy

About 80% of your business is generated by 20% of your clients. These 20% deserve special attention and fall under the category of "best" clients. These are the clients who come first with you. For example, if you are offered two projects from two different clients and you only have time to accept one of them, you accept the project from the "best" client. That doesn't mean you ignore the client who falls into the 80% category. You may be able to negotiate another deadline with him or her or come up with a compromise. But your priority is always to satisfy your "best" clients.

How do you keep your clients happy? Here are some recommendations for doing just that:

- Make sure that the quality of your work is terrific! Always do your best. This means safeguarding the excellence of more than just the quality of your products and services. It includes the excellence of your correspondence, the accuracy of your invoices, and the quality of every interaction, whether it be in person, via telephone, or via e-mail.
- A commitment to client satisfaction (and consistently excellent customer service) must be part of your company's mission, vision, and values. Include goals and objectives concerning client satisfaction as part of your action plan.

- Never promise something that you are not 100% sure you can deliver. If you don't have the skills or expertise to complete a project, refuse it. Clients will respect you for your honesty and business ethics.
- Never surprise a client with unexpected or bad news. Keep your client well-informed about the status of any project.
- Add value to your products and services. What can you do to make your business stand out from your competitors? Can you meet shorter deadlines? Consider offering "after hours" (e.g., evenings and weekends) sales support or availability.
- Always avoid any actual or even implied conflict of interest. A conflict of interest is a situation that puts your interests and your client's interests at odds. For example, suppose two of your clients are vying for the same health care research grant. Both of them want to hire you to write the application for this prestigious grant. Even though you may believe that you could write the applications for two competing clients without breaching confidentiality, it is a conflict of interest for you to work on behalf of both clients. Such behavior, if discovered, could significantly damage your business reputation. You may choose to accept the job from one of the clients (especially if one of them is a "best" client) or refuse both clients.
- Send a note or e-mail to clients at the completion of projects telling them how much you enjoyed working with them, that you value their business, and that you look forward to working with them again.

Another important way to keep your clients happy is by staying in touch with them, even when you are not currently working on projects for them. The trick is to stay in touch without becoming a nuisance.

Schedule specific days every month to "touch base" with your clients. If your clients are within driving distance, a breakfast or lunch meeting is a good option. However, the geographic distance between clients and entrepreneurs often makes such face-to-face meetings impossible. Phone calls and e-mail are useful communication tools when working with "long-distance" clients. If you call spontaneously, always ask the client if he or she has time to talk. Do not infringe on a client's time.

Don't call or e-mail "just to chat." When you communicate, be able to share information that is useful to the client. If you are e-mailing a client who is a nurse manager or director of nursing, attach an article on a relevant topic such as recruitment and retention or changes in accreditation mandates. A client who is responsible for grooming new managers may be pleased to learn about new ways to foster leadership and management skills. Do everything you can to make clients look forward to your phone calls and e-mails.

RECTIFYING YOUR MISTAKES

We all make mistakes and/or displease a client. If this happens, do whatever you can to satisfy your client, even if the mistake is not necessarily your fault. It is your responsibility to rectify mistakes and turn complaints into accolades. Remember, word-of-mouth can make or break an entrepreneur. An unhappy client will almost certainly tell other clients and potential clients that your work is unacceptable. Here are some actions to take when something goes wrong:

- Stay calm and objective. Avoid becoming defensive. Focus on your client's needs.
- Accept responsibility for your actions. Express willingness to solve problems. Propose specific actions to correct problems.
- Don't be afraid to apologize: "I regret any inconvenience this situation has caused."
- Take action promptly. As soon as you recognize a problem, initiate corrective action. Don't try to

hide, cover up, or blame someone else for your mistakes. Your client is more likely to be appeased by someone who accepts responsibility and works hard to correct problems.

- Follow-up promptly. Ask the client whether he or she is happy with the actions you've taken to correct the problem.

Red Alert

Underestimating the time it takes to complete a project is a common mistake made by new entrepreneurs. As you work on project, keep track of how you spend your time. Don't forget to include items such as telephone calls, research, and travel. These records will help you gauge your time more accurately. If you're just beginning your career as an entrepreneur, build in some extra time to complete projects. You'll probably find that the "extra" time isn't really extra at all!

DECIDING WHICH JOBS TO TAKE

Evaluate all project offers carefully prior to accepting them. The following table is designed to help you do that. Answer the questions with a "yes" or a "no." Your answer to each question will provide information to help you to make your decision.

Figure 6: Project Evaluation Survey

Record your answers by placing a check mark for yes or no.

	QUESTION	
1.	Do I have the skills and expertise to satisfactorily complete this project?	❏ Yes ❏ No
2.	Do I have the time to satisfactorily complete the project on time?	❏ Yes ❏ No
3.	Does the fee offered meet my requirements?	❏ Yes ❏ No

	QUESTIONS *Continued*	
4.	Do the client and I have compatible values, beliefs, and philosophies?	❑ Yes ❑ No
5.	Can I rely on the client to pay me promptly?	❑ Yes ❑ No
6.	Do I feel comfortable and communicate easily with the client?	❑ Yes ❑ No
7.	Does the client have a good reputation in the community and/or with other small business owners?	❑ Yes ❑ No
8.	Do I find the project interesting?	❑ Yes ❑ No
9.	Does the project have the potential to create additional entrepreneurial opportunities?	❑ Yes ❑ No
10.	Will this project allow me to expand my skills and knowledge?	❑ Yes ❑ No

HOW TO SAY "NO"

There are times when you need to refuse work. If you are refusing work from a client that you would like to work for in the future, be tactful. Say something like, "I would love to accept this project, but I'm fully booked at this time. I hope you'll call me again." You could also give a more specific reason for refusing such as not being able to meet the client's deadline. This way, you and the client may be able to compromise on another deadline that allows you to accept the project, or some version of it. However, if you really are unable to accept the project at all, don't hesitate to tactfully refuse.

If you are refusing work from a client that you really believe is not a good fit for you, refer him or her to another entrepreneur. The client will probably develop a working relationship with an entrepreneur who will remember that you sent business his or her way. Always be tactful and polite.

Red Alert ☢

If your intuition is telling
you that a problem exists
(even if you answer "yes" to all of the
preceding question) pay attention!
Take the time to further investigate
the potential client. Feeling uneasy
may mean that your instincts are
more accurate than the objective
questionnaire.

There are also times when you aren't sure that you can say "yes" but you really don't want to say "no." Ask the client if you could take some time to review the project. Tell the client when you will make your decision (e.g., "I'll call you by noon tomorrow") and stick to that deadline. Answer the questions on the Project Evaluation Survey (Figure 6), listen to your intuition, and make your decision. Don't keep a potential client waiting!

RECOGNIZING "PROBLEM" CLIENTS

New entrepreneurs are often tempted to accept any work offered to them! There are some jobs you should refuse to accept, no matter how much you need the work! Here are some warning signs to help you recognize "problem" clients:

- Problem clients ask you to develop a proposal free-of-charge. They say that this will help them to determine if you are the right person for their projects. What this usually means is they want your ideas and input but do not want to hire you.
- Problem clients complain and generally "bad mouth" other entrepreneurs, often identifying them by name. Not only is this unprofessional, but it lets you know that the clients will probably complain about you too.
- Problem clients supply you with excessive amounts of details and background information but won't discuss the project or identify goals and objectives. In this case, the client probably doesn't know what he or she wants and is likely to

disagree with anything you propose or blame you for any failures.

- Problem clients set unrealistic deadlines, propose inadequate fees, and/or refuse to negotiate or compromise. These clients are rigid, uncompromising, and just plain difficult.

When one or more of these warning signs surface, refuse the job.

GETTING FIRED

If you pursue your entrepreneurial life long enough, you'll probably be fired at least once. There are a number of reasons for which entrepreneurs are fired, and not all of them are related to your job performance.

Sometimes the client and his or her organization experience unexpected financial problems. These problems may result in the following situations:

- There is no longer enough money to pay you.
- Your projects are eliminated as part of a massive budget cut.
- The client's organization is reorganized and your projects are no longer considered a priority.

• Success Strategy • • • • • • • • • •

If you are fired in the middle of a project because of budgetary concerns, you may be entitled to receive payment for the work you've done depending on the wording of your contract or letter of agreement. You may want to structure your contracts and letters of agreement to deal with this possibility.

Budget cuts may also cause your main contact within an organization to lose his or her job. If this happens, your contact's projects may also be eliminated. Without a project, you have no job within this organization.

Red Alert

Don't align yourself too closely with any one person within an organization. Do not take sides in political disputes or negatively discuss anyone within an organization. The person you malign may be the next CEO!

Internal politics plays a role in all organizations. Suppose your main contact is reassigned or downsized. His or her replacement may not want to work with you because you have ties with someone who was downsized. Or it may simply be politically advantageous for the new person to work with another entrepreneur.

Finally, you may be fired due to inadequate performance—you failed to deliver products and services according to your client's expectations. Don't take it personally, and don't chastise yourself. Don't argue with the client and don't talk disparagingly about him or her to other business associates. Learn from your mistakes. If you are fired for inadequate performance:

- Take it as a reminder to review the quality of your work. Almost everyone becomes complacent at times. Use this unfortunate event as a trigger to set and meet higher standards.
- Take it as an opportunity to seek new projects with new clients.
- Take it as an incentive to seek new challenges.

FIRING A CLIENT

There are times when you simply cannot tolerate working for a particular client. But before you make the decision to "fire" a client think it over carefully. The following suggestions offer justifiable reasons to terminate your relationship with a client. It also identifies the times when you should *not* fire a client.

Valid Reasons for Firing a Client

- The client asks you to violate your professional business ethics.

- The client asks you to complete a project that is a blatant conflict of interest.
- The client fails to treat you politely and with respect.
- The client insists that you produce substandard work.

Red Alert

Never allow one client to supply the majority of your business income. If you and he or she do part company, the loss can be insurmountable. Diversify your clientele.

- The client consistently fails to pay you on time.
- The client pays you less than you are worth.
- The client keeps changing his or her mind about the goals and objectives of the project.

Valid Reasons to Think Twice Before Firing a Client

- The client is one of your best clients and is only causing problems during one project.
- The client is your primary source of income.
- The client is willing to negotiate and improve the working relationship.
- The client is a good referral source and recommends you to other clients.

Susan M. Drake, the author of *Freelancing for Dummies,* says that the best way to fire a client is to not let them know you fired them. It's best not to anger or embarrass any client. You may desire to work with them in the future and will not want to leave them with a bad impression of you or your work. Here are some tips for tactfully firing a client:

- Make yourself unavailable to them. Explain that you are fully booked and cannot work on their project until some time in the distant future. (Make sure that you emphasize the word "distant"). You may choose to recommend another entrepreneur.

- Ask for more money than the client is willing to pay. The client will either stop calling you, or if he or she really wants your services, will agree to your demands. (If the client is willing to pay you that much money, you may even want to consider accepting the project).
- Explain that you do not feel you are the best person to complete the project and you may choose to recommend another entrepreneur.

• Success Strategy

If you do recommend another entrepreneur, be sure to let him or her know that you have done so. Tactfully share the reasons you have refused to work for a particular client. Don't gossip or "bad mouth" the client. However, if the client is truly intolerable (e.g., unethical, disrespectful) don't recommend him or her to anyone else.

CONCLUSION

Client satisfaction is essential to your business. Your reputation and income depend on it. There are times when you and a client simply will not be able to work together. If so, don't chastise yourself, and don't alienate the client. Be professional when severing professional relationships.

RESOURCES

Allen, K. (2001). *Entrepreneurship for Dummies.* New York: Wiley Publishing.

Drake, S. M. (2001). *Freelancing for Dummies.* New York: Hungry Minds.

Edwards, P., Edwards, S., & Economy, P. (2000). *Home-Based Business for Dummies.* Foster City, CA: IDG Books.

THIRTEEN

Market Research and Client Identification

Client satisfaction, as discussed in chapter 12, depends in part on your identifying and obtaining the right clients. Market research, when properly conducted, helps you to identify your primary customers, determine the level of demand for your products and services, and identify appropriate pricing strategies. Failure to perform meaningful market research may lead to the demise of your business before you have a chance to get started!

UNDERSTANDING THE CONCEPT OF MARKET RESEARCH

Market research is, quite simply, the process of finding out if there is a market for your products and services and whether this market is large enough to support you. Most small businesses are able to sell at least some of their products and services. The big question is, "Will you be able to make enough money to earn a living?" Market research will help to answer that question.

Conducting market research is arguably the most important thing you can do before actually taking the "leap'" into entrepreneurship. Without market research you won't know how much competition you'll face, who your competition is, what the current market price is for services and products such as yours, where your customers are located, or how to reach them. Even if you believe that your products and services are of exceptional quality and desperately needed, what happens if nobody else does? Or what if potential customers think your products and services are terrific but not a necessity? In the current cost-conscious health care environment, your products and services must have measurable value. Do they improve patient safety, enhance patient outcomes, and/or improve job performance? Will they facilitate adherence to accreditation standards? Are they affordable? You won't know the answers to these questions unless you do your market research.

Some new entrepreneurs ask if they should conduct their own market research or if they should hire a professional marketing firm. Hiring a marketing firm is beyond the budget of most fledgling entrepreneurs. It is probably in your best interest to conduct your own market research. Here are several helpful Web sites for the entrepreneur conducting market research:

- Health Data Insights: Its mission is to "revolutionize health care by transforming it into a market-and-consumer-driven business through the provision of actionable intelligence." This site provides a wealth of information on the health care market including products and services, surveys, and relevant statistics. Visit them at **www.healthmarketinsights.com.**
- American Demographics: They provide extensive information on consumer markets. Visit them at **www.demographics.com.**
- American Association for Public Opinion Research: This site covers a wide variety of statistics concerning public views on issues of general interest. Reach them at **www.aapor.org.**
- United States Census Bureau. This is the official resource for social demographics and economic statistics. They are at **www.census.gov.**
- Web Side Story. This site provides Internet statistics, user trends, raw data, and free analysis. Visit them at **www.websidestory.com.**

How do you logically conduct market research? There are three basic components of market research: analysis of your market, analysis of your competitors, and testing your market.

MARKET ANALYSIS

There are two types of market analysis: primary research and secondary research. (Despite its name, you do your secondary research first.) Secondary research is the process of finding out what consumers say about products and services similar to yours and why and how they purchase them. Explore appropriate Web sites, read newspapers and journals, and pay attention to the news and financial reports broadcast on television and radio. Trade associations and your local library are also good resources. When you conduct secondary research, you are looking for:

- competitors who provide products and services similar to yours, how much they charge, and to whom they sell,
- consumers of products and services similar to yours, how much they pay for them, and from whom they purchase.

After you complete your secondary research you are ready to conduct your primary research. Conducting your own research on potential clients in your target market in person and via survey is referred to as primary research. *Target market* is defined as the body of customers who are most likely to purchase your products and services. It is important that you obtain data from potential customers who are objective and unbiased. Do not rely solely on input from family, friends, and close colleagues. These people want to support you and build up your confidence, but you can not rely on the impartiality of their responses.

Choose a representative sample of your target market comprised of people who have no vested interest in seeing you succeed or fail. Choose individuals who are able to give you honest feedback. If possible, interview these people in person.

Red Alert

Do not arrive unannounced at the offices of potential clients. Arrange a mutually convenient time to meet. When setting up an appointment tell the potential client the purpose of your visit, what types of products and services you provide, and how these products and services can benefit the client.

In reality, you will probably acquire most of your information via telephone and written surveys. These types of surveys are fairly easy to implement and have the advantage of reaching many people (more people than you can reach via personal visits). However, there are problems associated with such surveys. Kathleen Allen, in *Entrepreneurship for Dummies,* identifies the following disadvantages of marketing surveys conducted by mail or telephone:

- Developing good questionnaires is a challenge.
- The response to mail surveys is generally low, only around 15%.
- With mail and telephone surveys, you do not have the benefit of observing nonverbal communication. Nonverbal clues can be critical since studies indicate that 85% of all communication is nonverbal.
- It is difficult to clarify responses to written surveys.
- Studies indicate that telephone surveys are time-consuming and prone to interviewer bias.

Success Strategy

You may also choose to conduct surveys via e-mail. However, most computers are equipped to delete messages interpreted as spam. Additionally, busy potential clients may simply delete your e-mail without reading it or even be annoyed that you sent it.

Despite the disadvantages, for practical reasons, you need to use both mail (e-mail and postal mail) and telephone surveys to gather the information you want. Here are some suggestions for the development of surveys.

- Keep the survey brief. Limit the survey to 5-10 questions. Keep the questions short and simple.
- Do not ask leading or biased questions such as, "Do you think you are paying too much for products and services?"
- Minimize the number of open-ended questions. These questions take considerable time to answer and can lack focus. People are more likely to complete a survey that is easy and takes little time to complete.
- Ask the easiest questions first.
- When asking multiple choice questions do not give more than four choices.

The following sample survey (Figure 7) incorporates the preceding suggestions. It is written by a hypothetical management consultant.

Figure 7: Sample Market Research Survey

Thank you for completing this written survey.

I am a management consultant specializing in the development of managers and leaders who motivate their employees, enhance job performance, and improve patient outcomes. The purpose of this survey is to identify your management and leadership needs and determine how I can help you meet them. Please circle the letter before the responses that best describe your needs and mail it back to me in the enclosed, postage paid envelope.

1. How often do you require management and leadership training?
   a. monthly   b. quarterly
   c. annually   d. other_____

2. What is your primary source for providing such training?
   a. in-house staff development department
   b. self-learning tools such as videos or computer-based learning
   c. consultants
   d. other_____

3. How much money do you spend on management/leadership training annually?
   a. less than $5,000   b. between $5,000-$10,000
   c. between $10,000-$20,000   d. other_____

4. Do you currently outsource management/leadership training?
   ___Yes   ___No

5. What types of management/leadership training are you most interested in offering to your employees?
   _____
   _____
   _____

After gathering your data for market analysis, it's time to analyze your competition.

COMPETITOR ANALYSIS

Start with competitors located within your visiting distance. When possible, visit the businesses, talk to the people who work there, and interview people who purchase products and services from them. Read local newspapers and listen to local television and radio stations to gather information about their sales techniques.

Do an Internet search. Type in the name of your business competitors and see what pops up. There are also some useful Web sites to help you analyze your competition.

- NewsDirectory.com: This site provides access to Web sites of thousands of publications and is found at **www.newsdirectory.com**.
- Inc500: This site offers advice, tools, and services that help entrepreneurs start, run, and market their businesses and is found at **www.Inc.com**.
- U. S. Securities & Exchange Commission: If your competitors are publicly traded, they must file annual and quarterly reports with the U. S. Securities and Exchange Commission. You can research them at **www.sec.gov**.
- ProfNet: This site offers direct links to business experts at corporations, colleges, universities, and national laboratories and is found at **www.profnet.com**.

Keep a record of your competitors, how they market themselves, the quality of their products, and anything else that you find useful. Update the list with new competitors as you find them and keep track of "old" competitors so that your information stays as current as possible.

MARKET TESTING

Market testing helps us assess the market's reaction to new products and services. This is done at an early stage in the development of your business before a complete and expensive commitment is made to your new career. It helps you gain important information about the likelihood of success of your products and services.

Hingston and Balfour in *Working from Home* identify several strategies for market testing.

- Advertise: Create a stimulating advertisement or series of advertisements and evaluate customer response.
- Sampling: Take a sample of your products and services and sell them for a limited time or take them (as a vendor) to trade shows and conventions.
- Focus Groups: Selected clients (or potential clients) are invited to preview specific new products and services or prototypes of your products and services and evaluate customer response.
- Mail: Send letters or brochures to potential clients asking them to evaluate the potential of your products and services. Enclose a stamped, self-addressed envelop for them to return their responses when using postal mail.

Be aware of the most common mistakes made by those conducting market research. They include the following:

- asking biased questions
- ignoring the results of your research (especially if it's something you don't want to hear)
- ignoring the strength of your competition
- failing to realize that 80% of your business comes from 20% of your clients
- failing to "listen" to clients and potential clients
- underestimating the length of time and the amount of planning it takes to establish a business

CONCLUSION

Market research is an on-going process. Schedule specific times to collect new data and analyze it in terms of its impact on your business. In fact, schedule time to conduct market research on a monthly basis!

RESOURCES

Allen, K. (2001). *Entrepreneurship for Dummies.* New York: Wiley Publishing.

Drake, S. M. (2001). *Freelancing for Dummies.* New York: Hungry Minds.

Hingston, P., & Balfour, A. (2001). *Working from Home.* New York: Dorling Kindersley.

FOURTEEN

Marketing Strategies

There as many ways to market businesses as there are entrepreneurs. The secret is to find the ways that are effective for you and are within your marketing budget. Research how products and services such as yours are normally marketed. What kinds of marketing tactics attract you? What kinds of marketing tactics repel you?

The basic foundation of your marketing efforts is really two-fold. First determine how your clients most effectively learn about products and services like yours. Then calculate how much you can afford to spend on marketing strategies.

SELECTING MARKETING TOOLS

The first question to answer is, "How are my customers most likely to be reached?" For example, if you sell health care related novelties such as tote bags, pens, clothing, etc., it wouldn't make much sense to advertise solely in local newspapers unless your paper happens to reach many thousands of health care workers. Consider creating a small catalogue of your products and mailing it to your target clients.

As your business grows and revenue increases, explore the possibility of a wider mailing list and a business Web site. Web sites are becoming more and more common and the costs of developing them are decreasing. Purchase vendor space (if economically feasible) from professional health care associations and sell your products at their conventions and conferences. On the other hand, if you are offering holistic health interventions such as massage, guided imagery, or classes in Tai Chi, local advertising may be the perfect option for you. A savvy entrepreneur determines the costs of specific types of marketing and the effectiveness of various strategies, and then selects the best, most cost-effective marketing strategy for his or her business.

Radio, Television, and Journal Advertising

Radio and television advertising are expensive ways to advertise a new business. Effective media advertising is also long-term by nature. Most consumers need to hear or see advertisements several times before they respond. So any media-based advertising campaign must be long-term.

If you have the financial resources, and your particular business is best served by media advertising, obtain the services of media professionals. Few people are able to present themselves effectively on radio or television without any coaching. Listen to radio and observe television advertisements. What makes some of them effective and others dismal failures? Tone of voice, delivery style, and appearance on camera strongly influence the impression viewers and listeners form of you and your business.

Consider the types of businesses most likely to benefit from radio and television advertising. Television advertising is realistically not the best form of marketing for most fledgling nurse entrepreneurs. It is expensive and it is doubtful that enough business would be generated by it to justify the expense.

Radio, however, is often helpful as a local marketing strategy. If you are selling products and services from a specific geographic location, radio advertising makes sense. Suppose you are running a boutique that specializes in clothing, wigs, and make-up tips for persons undergoing chemotherapy or other appearance-changing treatment. This is an excellent example of a business that could benefit from radio advertising.

Advertising in professional journals is another option. The types of products and services advertised, as well as the cost of the advertisement vary among journals. If you are interested in reaching particular populations of health care professionals, consider marketing your business in appropriate professional publications.

Vendor Exhibitor

Exhibiting your products and services at conventions, conferences, and continuing education programs can be a costly but effective means of marketing. Organizations and associations sell exhibit space to vendors as a way of offsetting the costs of major events. National conferences and conventions reach large numbers of people, but you can count on spending a minimum of $1,000 to secure space as a vendor. This does not include the costs of transportation, lodging, and shipping the materials that are part of your exhibit.

There are options other than major conferences and conventions. Health care organizations and local affiliates of professional organizations often plan meetings and education programs for local audiences, and sometimes they sell exhibit space as well. The cost of exhibiting at these types of events is probably well within your marketing budget. The number of persons in attendance is not large, but local (within driving distance) events can provide you with a venue to market your business in a relatively cost-effective manner.

Local Marketing

Newspapers are also good sources for businesses to target local markets, and they are relatively cost-effective. Cost varies with size, number of lines, the style of the ad, and its graphics. Before writing your advertisement, carefully read the newspapers in which you hope to advertise and critique the marketing ads objectively. Decide what you like (and dislike) about the ads. You'll get some of your best ideas by reviewing the marketing strategies of other entrepreneurs.

Use your skill and ingenuity to identify cost-free ways of marketing your business. For example, if you participate in or sponsor a charity event, ask that your business name be included in promotional materials. If you are able to contribute financially to an event you may ask that you be identified by your business name: "The Hazleton Chapter of the American Cancer Society thanks Holistic Nursing Care, Erica Reynolds, President, for sponsoring today's luncheon."

Volunteer to present an educational program (free of charge) at local senior citizens centers, public libraries, etc. Choose a topic that interests a broad audience (e.g., blood pressure reduction, "heart healthy" diets, etc.). These types of programs are publicized free of charge in a variety of ways, including newspapers and health care community publications. Be sure to give program sponsors one of your business cards so that they can refer your products and services to others.

Red Alert

Don't abuse this type of opportunity. If you are presenting a 30 minute program on heart healthy diets do not use 15 of those minutes as a "commercial" for your business. This offends the audience and the program sponsor and you will lose rather than gain clients. You may mention your business when you introduce yourself, but that should be the extent of your self-promotion.

Community newsletters can be a really good source of publicity. Most towns and cities have at least one newsletter devoted to community events and are happy to publicize your volunteer efforts. Such newsletters also sell advertising space that is usually less expensive than traditional newspaper advertising.

There are a few organizations that can help you develop your marketing strategies as well as network with business contacts. They include the following:

- Your local Chamber of Commerce probably has a small business division. For more information about Chamber activities and services, and to

locate the chapter closest to you, contact
www.chamberofcommerce.com.

- The American Small Business Association is another excellent resource for small business owners and can be reached at **www.asbaonline.org**.
- The National Association of Home Based Businesses exists to help home-based businesses survive and thrive. Contact this organization at **www.usahomebusiness.com.**
- Le Tip is an interesting organization that might be helpful for some entrepreneurs. Its purpose is to "exchange business tips." Members meet to network and share referrals. Le Tip eliminates competition among chapter members by making sure that each business category is represented by only one member, and conflicts of interest are disallowed. In other words, if you are a health care management consultant you would be the only such consultant in your local Le Tip chapter. No other health care management consultant would be allowed membership unless you choose to leave the chapter. For more information and to locate the Le Tip chapter closest to you contact **www.letip.com**.

Publishing and Public Speaking

One of the best ways to publicize your business is as an author. Submit articles to professional journals. Present a paper at a convention or conference. Although you usually will not earn money for these activities, they give you fantastic opportunities to network and publicize your business.

Brochures

There are numerous software programs that help you to develop and produce high-quality promotional materials on your own computer. Go to a reliable office supply store and ask for recommendations and assistance in choosing your software. Here are some tips for the development of promotional materials.

- Design a prototype/template (even if you draw it by hand) of the marketing materials you want to develop. It will help the computer software salespeople select the software most appropriate for your needs.

- Identify the quantity of brochures and other materials you need to create and reproduce. Use the data from your market research to help you come up with an accurate count.

- Calculate the maximum amount of money you can spend on developing and distributing promotional materials and stick to it!

Business Cards

• *Success Strategy* • • • • • • • • • • • •

The first step of your marketing strategy is to have business cards printed and carry some with you EVERYWHERE you go. You never know where and when you will have an opportunity to network. Lucrative business deals can be made at the supermarket, while jogging, or when attending your child's soccer game!

Your business cards must be attractive and professional. There are software packages available that allow you to design and print your own business cards. If you are not comfortable with this option, head for your local office supply store. They have a huge variety of styles and graphics to choose from and you can purchase a large number of cards very inexpensively. A word of caution: You are responsible for the layout and accuracy of the information on your business cards. Type or print this information. The office supply store employees will not proofread your work for you. If you spell your name or street incorrectly that is how it will appear on your business cards. Proofread your work carefully and ask a family member or friend to proofread it too!

Your business cards must look crisp and professional. Don't go overboard with colors and graphics. A border of colorful flowers is not appropriate for a management consultant. Include a brief phrase that conveys what it is that your business does. Review the business cards of colleagues and the samples available at the office supply store. Search the Internet by typing "business cards" into your search engine. Before having your cards printed ask a professional colleague for an objective critique of your ideas. Your business cards should include your name and title, your business name and address, a phrase describing your business, phone, fax, and e-mail information.

Web Site Development

Developing your own Web site is not as complicated or expensive as it once was. If you are thinking about developing a Web site, get professional assistance. A Web site must be easy to navigate, professional in both appearance and content, and easy to update. Here are some suggestions to follow as you contemplate developing your own Web site.

- First, surf the Internet and check out Web sites that contain elements you'd like to incorporate into your own site. Keep a record of what you like and what you dislike about various sites.
- Remember that ease of navigation is a priority! If you are selling products and services online, include online ordering options too.
- Research companies specializing in Web site design. Your local chamber of commerce will be able to help you locate such companies. You may choose to work with online companies that specialize in helping small business owners design Web sites. An example is Instant Site Design (**www.instantsitedesign.com**). Just search the

Internet for "Web site design" and you'll receive a huge amount of information. Ask the designers you are thinking of hiring for references. Review other Web sites that they've designed and talk to the small business owners who hired them.

- When you're ready to launch your Web site, you'll need to host it on a computer that is connected to the Internet 24 hours a day, seven days a week. The companies that help you design your site will also have information about hosting companies.
- Register your site on major registry services.
- Include your Web site address on all promotional materials and on your business cards.
- Send e-mail, regular mail, and in-person notifications to key groups of clients and potential clients announcing the launch of your Web site.

WRITING A MARKETING PLAN

The basic components of a marketing plan are:
- purpose
- overview
- objectives
- market analysis
- marketing strategies
- financial concepts

As a small business owner your marketing plan will probably be fairly brief. You may even be able to include it in its entirety as part of your business plan. As your business grows it may become necessary to develop a more detailed, extensive marketing plan. In this case, simply provide an overview of your market strategies in your business plan and write a more detailed marketing plan as a separate document.

Purpose

The *purpose* component to your marketing plan tells the reader what it is your business accomplishes. For example, the purpose of a business that focuses on management and leadership training might be: "to create name recognition and awareness in the marketplace where target clients are defined as health care organizations dealing with the challenges of management in the 21st century."

When you write your marketing purpose, look at your business from your clients' prospective. What would make you want to purchase your business's products and services. What would deter you from making these purchases?

The purpose is not lengthy or verbose. Make it concise, objective, and easily understood.

Overview

The overview is a brief summary of your overall marketing plan. It covers the essentials of your marketing focus, strategies, products and services, your marketing budget, and your projected revenue.

Marketing Objectives

Objectives should be as specific as possible. For example, a revenue-related objective is, "30% of revenue will come from contracts with health care organizations X and Y." This kind of specificity helps you to design marketing strategies aimed directly at achieving your marketing objectives. They also act as benchmarks by which you can measure the accuracy of your market research and evaluate the success of your marketing efforts.

Market Analysis

Market analysis is an overview of the results of your market research. Include the following information in your market analysis:

- the demographics of your client population

- the demographics of your competitors
- economic and social trends that influence your business and your clients
- technological trends that influence the way you and your clients conduct business
- the products and services of your competitors, their strengths, and weaknesses
- an overview of your products and services and how they compare to those of your competitors

Marketing Strategies

Your marketing strategies must directly address your marketing objectives. Identify at least one marketing strategy for every objective. Include the following items in your strategy description:

- the characteristics of your products and services that make it easy to market them (Characteristics might include impact on patient care, job performance, or patient satisfaction. If your products and services ultimately improve nurses' job performance, use that as a key marketing point.)
- a brief overview of your pricing strategies
- how you market your business (e.g., Web site, brochures, radio, etc.)
- an explanation of how your products and services are delivered to your customers

Financial Concepts

This section describes your financial picture for a fiscal year. For ease of understanding, you can present this information either monthly or quarterly. In this section, identify anticipated revenue and growth percentages. Explicitly calculate the costs of your marketing efforts such as the cost of developing and distributing brochures, the manufacture of products and services, or the cost of exhibiting at a convention or conference.

CONCLUSION

Marketing your products and services is the cornerstone of your business. A carefully designed and meticulously implemented marketing plan is essential. Rely on the objective data you gather and use these findings to effectively share your business products and services with your target clientele.

RESOURCES

Avillion, A. E. (2003). *Writing a Staff Development Plan: Business Strategies for the 21*[st] *Century.* Pensacola, FL: National Nursing Staff Development Organization (NNSDO).

Edwards, P., Edwards, S., & Economy, P. (2000). *Home-Based Business for Dummies.* Foster City, CA: IDG Books.

Lesonsky, R. (2004). *Start Your Own Business.* Canada: Entrepreneur Press.

Unit Five

ESTABLISHING A SERIOUS BUSINESS ENVIRONMENT

FIFTEEN

The Non-Home Office

Entrepreneurs generally have two choices when it comes to setting up their offices: the home office or the non-home office. There are advantages and disadvantages to both options. The non-home office is usually not the first office setting established by nurse entrepreneurs. It is generally too expensive and probably not necessary for the majority of small businesses established by nurses. Base your decision of where to set up your office on zoning and licensing regulations as well as the type of business you intend to run.

CRITERIA FOR A NON-HOME OFFICE

- **The nature of your business:** Will clients be coming to your business office in order to purchase your products and services? Consider, for example, the case of a nurse entrepreneur who is running a Holistic Care business. Jean offers relaxation training, Tai Chi classes, stress management techniques, and therapeutic massage. She needs space to conduct these various activities as well as a reception area staffed by a secretary. There must also be adequate parking space and an entrance ramp for mobility-challenged clients. She lives in a residential development. It is obvious that Jean's business requires a non-home office.

- **Zoning and licensing regulations:** If zoning and licensing regulations in your neighborhood forbid the establishment of a home-office, your business must be run from another location.
- **Entrepreneurial preference:** Some entrepreneurs prefer not to deal with the distractions associated with working from home.
- **Client preference:** Some clients may not take home-based entrepreneurs seriously. Although this rarely occurs, you may encounter these feelings depending on your clientele. Brenda is a performance coach. Her clients are health care CEOs and other members of administrative teams. Although she does most of her work on site at various health care organizations, she also meets clients in her office. While it is common for performance coaches to work from home, Brenda's clientele is likely to expect her to have an office that reflects their own work standards and level of achievement.

ESTABLISHING A NON-HOME OFFICE

First calculate the maximum amount of money you have available to rent or purchase and maintain office space. The majority of entrepreneurs will rent rather than buy office space. Renting office space is generally a fairly expensive proposition. To reduce expenses consider:

- sharing facilities and equipment with other office building tenants
- leasing rather than buying office equipment
- sharing space with a business that is compatible with yours, but does not compete with it. (In a best-case scenario, you may even be able to share referrals.)

- bartering with services instead of cash (For example, you may be able to receive a discount on your Web site design if you agree to refer the designer to a number of other entrepreneurs.)

• Success Strategy ••••••••••••••

Consider all potential costs. Remember to include utilities in your budget. Find out if any utilities are included in your rent. Find out how trash is removed. Consider whether you need to make arrangements for hazardous waste disposal. Consider who will clean your office.

Determine architectural, permit, licensing, and safety issues. Answer the following questions:

- Does your business location require adaptations to adhere to accessibility standards?
- Is there sufficient parking space close to your office?
- If you are conducting business after dark, is the parking area equipped with enough lights?
- Is your office located in a safe neighborhood? Do you need to install a security system?
- Have you determined what types of permits and licenses your business requires? Have you checked with community officials and your business accountant about these requirements?
- If you are hiring employees, are you familiar with labor relations standards? Do you have written job descriptions and policies and procedures? Do you have a written disciplinary action procedure? Is there a grievance procedure in place?
- Are smoke alarms and carbon monoxide alarms in place?

Success Strategy

In your previous role, you may have hated the politics and challenges of supervising others. But if you hire or plan to hire a staff you need to have all of the guidelines in place to supervise others. Don't assume that a two or three person business operation does not need job descriptions, dress codes, grievance procedures, etc.

Establish working hours. Hours of operation depend on your products and services.

- What hours are convenient for your clients? If you are offering services such as relaxation training, your hours of operation will probably include evenings and weekends. Your market research will tell you who your clients will be and when they will use your products and services. A performance coach, for example, needs to be available during the hours his or her clients are working (primarily during the day) although some evening availability may be expected.

- Be sure that your family and friends understand your business hours. If you let them believe that as an entrepreneur, your evenings and weekends are free, you're going to run into trouble. Even if your clients interact with you during the day, you'll need to catch up on paper work, networking, etc., during evening hours and on weekends.

- Who will operate your business when you are ill or on vacation? Will your business close during these times? Do you expect your employee(s) to take their vacations when you take yours? Do you have a partner or partners? How will you schedule vacations and other absences?

How will you and your staff dress for success?

- No matter how small your business is, consider instituting a dress code. Will you or others wear uniforms or lab coats when providing services? Do you plan on limiting the use of jewelry or make-up? If you and your employees plan to wear street clothes, have you determine what is and what is not appropriate? Is your dress code in writing?
- A client's first impression of your appearance is important. A vice-president of nursing who visits your office will not be impressed if your secretary greets her in blue jeans, wearing a large nose ring, and chewing gum. On the other hand, clients coming to attend a Tai Chi course may be uncomfortable if you appear in a sophisticated business suit. But no matter what type of business you operate, staff should be dressed in clean, neat clothes and behave in a professional, respectful manner.

Red Alert

Remember that dressing for success also applies when you visit clients or vendors at their offices. Find out what the "norm" is for individual businesses. If you're unsure, dress conservatively. It's better to attend a meeting in a business suit even if, to your surprise, your CEO client is in blue jeans, than it is to arrive in blue jeans and find that everyone else is attired in business clothes.

What resources do you need? For the non-home office, what resources do you need that are specific to your business?

- Consider the décor of your office. If your business specializes in stress reduction techniques avoid loud, stimulating colors such as red. Consult decorating books to determine the color scheme best suited to your business. Painting the walls of your business is an inexpensive way to create the atmosphere you want.

- Consider the needs of your clients. Will your clients have mobility problems? Will clients in wheelchairs be able to navigate throughout your office? What types of chairs will be most comfortable for your clients?
- Explore office furniture outlets when purchasing desks, chairs, file cabinets, etc. These outlets often have excellent products for sale at very reasonable prices.
- How many telephones will you need? Make sure that you have telephones with "speaker phone" capability. These may also be purchased inexpensively at outlets and bargain stores.
- What type of Internet access is available for your office? Select the fastest, most reliable access available. Your ability to conduct Internet research and communicate with others via e-mail is absolutely imperative! Don't be afraid to spend money on Internet services and your e-mail provider. This is one area that deserves special attention!
- How many computers will you need? How many printers will you need? What types of software will you need? Will you need to track sales, orders, and deliveries? Will you need to maintain schedules of appointments, classes, and mailing lists? How will you track payroll?

CONCLUSION

However, if you determine that the non-home office is your best option, proceed cautiously. Consider all of the factors identified in this chapter and seek advice from your local Chamber of Commerce and other small business owners. Don't limit your contacts to owners of health care related businesses. Many of the problems encountered by small business owners are the same, regardless of the type of business they operate.

RESOURCES

Allen, K. (2001). *Entrepreneurship for Dummies.* New York: Wiley Publishing.

Drake, S. M. (2001). *Freelancing for Dummies.* New York: Hungry Minds.

Edwards, P., Edwards, S., & Economy, P. (2000). *Home-Based Business for Dummies.* Foster City, CA: IDG Books.

SIXTEEN

The Home Office

Most entrepreneurs start their businesses from the comfort of a home office. A home office can be the most wonderful location from which to run a business—or it can be a misery. Here are some recommendations for the establishment of a home office.

ADVANTAGES AND DISADVANTAGES OF THE HOME OFFICE

Advantages

- Home offices are inexpensive. Setting up an office in an existing space in your home costs you far less than renting an office and paying for its maintenance, utilities, and renovations.
- Home offices are convenient. You no longer have to commute on crowded highways. If you need to work late at night you don't have to worry about being alone in a deserted office building or driving on lonely highways.
- Home offices facilitate time management. The time you formerly spent on commuting can now be used to finish a project or do your grocery shopping on a weekday afternoon instead of on Saturday morning.
- Home offices provide you with tax advantages. A home office deduction can save you money and

facilitate your cash flow. Talk to your accountant about home office deductions.

Disadvantages

- Working at home may make you vulnerable to the demands of family and friends. They may believe that since you are at home all day you are available to run errands, act as a babysitter, and perform numerous other tasks for people with "real" jobs.
- Working at home offers a number of distractions. You may find yourself eating more than usual because the kitchen is right down the hall. Turning on the television or radio is a very tempting idea. And wouldn't you love to call your best friend to share your latest news? It takes a lot of discipline to work from home.
- Working at home is more difficult if you can't find (or don't have) the right space for an office.
- Working at home may tempt you to perform household chores during work hours.

SETTING LIMITS

Don't go out of your way to tell extended family, friends, and neighbors that you are about to work from home. The minute you do so, some of them will become convinced that you are available to act as babysitter, chauffeur, and errand runner. You will be the first person they call if they need someone to "let the plumber in" (and stay in the house until the plumber finishes) or to accept deliveries throughout the day while they are at work *away* from home. This doesn't mean you can't help out during an emergency. But you've got to let these people know that even though your office is in your house you are still working full-time and have duties, obligations, and office hours, just like everyone else. This may cause some friction at first, but setting limits is essential to your success as an entrepreneur.

You also need to set limits with your immediate family. They may assume you are now able to run all of the errands you used to reserve for weekends. Set up the same type of "errand sharing" schedule you had when you worked for someone else. If you didn't share these types of responsibilities before, now is a good time to start. Remember, your work hours during the early entrepreneurial years are going to increase, not decrease.

Another mistake young entrepreneurs (and their spouses) with small children often make is to assume that daycare or preschool is no longer needed. There is no way you can take care of your children all day while attempting to start a business. Their needs will naturally come first, and your business will probably fail.

Your home office is your place of business. Treat it like one. Set these kinds of limits before you actually start your business and stick to them. Help your family and friends to realize why these limits are necessary. If they want you to succeed, they'll understand!

CHOOSING THE LOCATION OF YOUR HOME OFFICE

If possible, choose a room with a door that can be closed and locked. Examples of such a room include a guest room, loft, attic, or basement. Avoid locating your office next to the kitchen or noisy family room. Natural light may prove important to your sense of well-being. If possible, establish your office in a room with windows.

What happens if you don't have a guest room or similar space available? In that case, set up an office in a corner of your finished basement or den. Purchase an inexpensive decorative screen and use it as a "wall" to separate your office from the rest of the room.

If you expect clients to visit your office, avoid having

Red Alert

NEVER keep a television in your office. It's one of the worst possible distractions!

them walk through a messy kitchen or rooms and hallways strewn with newspapers, children's toys, and other clutter. Likewise, your office should not be cluttered with children's backpacks, your knitting, or other personal items. This does not project an image of a serious entrepreneur. Even if you never invite clients to your office, keep it clutter free. Personal clutter is too much of a distraction.

Success Strategy

If you set up your office in the attic or basement space, make sure the space has adequate light and ventilation and is clean and relatively clutter-free.

Here are some simple tips when choosing the location of your office:

- Your office must be located in an area with adequate privacy and security.
- Your office must possess enough light and be well ventilated and temperature controlled.
- Your office must have adequate storage space.
- Your office must be wired (or able to be wired) for phone service and Internet connections (preferably the highest speed Internet access in your area).

Success Strategy

If possible, do not store your business materials anywhere but in your office. If your files, inventory, etc., exceed your office space and any available space in your attic or garage, consider renting storage space elsewhere. Don't let you business take over your home; don't let your home take over your office.

EQUIPPING YOUR HOME OFFICE

Office Furniture

Sturdy, attractive office furniture does not need to be expensive. Explore office furniture outlets and compare prices and quality between outlets and office supply stores. Here are some "must have" pieces of office furniture.

- **Desk:** Your desk will get a lot of use. Choose one that is sturdy. If you have enough space, buy a large desk that can hold your computer monitor, keyboard, telephone, and more.
- **File Cabinets:** Although computers have replaced the need for many types of hard copy files, you still need at least two file cabinets. These should be sturdy and offer ample storage space. File cabinets can hold supplies such as envelopes, pens, etc., as well as files. Most home offices are not exceptionally large, so think of ways to make your office furniture do "double duty."
- **Bookshelves:** In addition to your reference books, your bookshelves can hold phone books, directories, and attractive boxes that house small office supplies such as stamps and address books.
- **Desk Chair:** You may be able to purchase bargain bookshelves and file cabinets, but buy the best chair that you can afford. You'll spend a lot of time in this chair working on your computer, talking on the telephone, and developing products and services. Your

Red Alert

Do not use your office furniture for anything but your business. Don't let your children do their homework at your desk or your spouse use your business phone for personal calls. Don't run the risk of missing important business calls or losing important paperwork because the whole family uses your office as a family room.

chair should be comfortable, sturdy, ergonomically correct, and adjustable to suit your height. (For information on ergonomically correct office furniture, visit **www.ergopro.com**.)

Telephone

If possible, your business phone number and personal phone number should be different. If you can't afford two distinct telephone lines in your home consider using your cell phone as your business phone. Using your cell phone has the added advantage of being able to travel with you wherever you go. There are many payment options available and it may be more economical for you to use your cell phone for your business.

Your office telephone should be capable of functioning as a speaker phone. Even if the exact nature of your business makes it unlikely that you will have to participate in conference calls, a speaker phone is relatively inexpensive and having one keeps the option open for you. You can purchase a speaker phone at office supply stores or bargain discount stores. The following telephone services are also recommended:

- caller ID
- call waiting
- call forwarding
- call-back

Red Alert

Do NOT allow your children to record your business message. Not only is it unprofessional, it may very well be unintelligible. Clients hearing a garbled version of twinkle, twinkle little star followed by an indecipherable message will not take you or your business seriously.

You'll need voice mail or an answering machine to pick up calls when you are not available. Record a short message such as: *"You have reached D.E.P. Management Consultants. We are unable to take your call at the present time. Please leave your name, number, and a brief message, and your call will be returned within 24 hours."*

Fax Machines

The cost of fax machines has decreased to the extent that nearly anyone can afford one. Even inexpensive fax machines now also often perform multiple tasks. You may find one that also functions as a scanner, copier, and answering machine. Visit your local office supply store and find one that best suits your needs and your budget.

• Success Strategy • • • • • • • • • • • • • • •

Consider purchasing a copier if your business mandates that you make multiple copies of lengthy documents. If you only need to make a few copies of short documents on an irregular basis, however, a copier is probably a waste of your money. Instead, look into printers and fax machines that have copying capabilities.

Computers

If you do not already have a computer designated for your use only, it is essential that you purchase a desktop computer. It is amazing, and rather frightening, that a significant number of nurses still resist learning to use a computer. You cannot function as a small business owner without a computer as well as Internet access. Your business computer should be used exclusively for your business. If your daughter uses it to research a history term paper and your husband uses it to access your joint e-mail account, you run the risk of having them view confidential client information, destroying important documents, and interfering with your work time. The family computer and your business computer must be two separate machines. Your business e-mail account must also be separate from the family account.

• Success Strategy • • • • • • • • • • • • • •

Limit access to your business computer by protecting it with a password.

Computer upgrade options seem to appear almost daily. You won't be able to afford every upgrade you see, but you also don't need every upgrade on the market. Find a computer specialist who is willing to serve as your computer consultant. He or she will help you decide what computer to buy, what programs you need, and what software to purchase. Your computer consultant can also help you select a monitor, printer, and scanner and advise you about upgrades and when it's time to purchase a new computer. Purchase the best possible computer in terms of power and memory but don't worry about the "extras" unless you really need them. For example, if you are going to use your computer primarily for word processing and Internet searches, you probably won't need extensive graphic design programs. Get the best of what you need and ignore the rest.

If you travel a lot you may need to purchase a laptop or notebook computer. Some laptops are so sophisticated you may not need a desktop model. Again, consult with your computer consultant to make the best possible purchasing decisions.

For the nurse entrepreneur, Internet access is essential. Avoid using your regular phone line unless it's separate from your personal and business lines. Telephone line connections are slow and can be precarious. Consider more reliable, high speed options such as cable connections. Remember also, that if you use either a cable connection or DSL line you'll be "online" around the clock. In this case you need to install a firewall on your computer. A firewall helps prevent hackers from accessing your computer.

Red Alert

ALWAYS back up your computer documents on CDs or disks.

Finally, computers function best in a clean environment that is maintained at a moderate temperature. Magnets can erase computerized data, so keep any type of magnetized material away from your computer. Use surge protectors to protect your computer from sudden electrical power bursts.

CREATING A COMFORTABLE HOME OFFICE

You're going to spend a lot of time in your home office. Create the most comfortable, ergonomically correct, and attractive space possible. Here are some suggestions for your comfort.

- Make your office inviting. Hang pictures on the walls, display personal mementos, and/or add a touch of greenery with easy maintenance live plants.
- Install the best lighting you can afford. If possible, situate your desk so that natural light from a window brightens your work space. If electric lighting is inadequate, bring in more lamps and/or have an electrician install more lighting options. Eyestrain and excessive fatigue are often due to working in a poorly lit environment.
- Your office must be climate controlled and adequately ventilated.
- Your office furniture should be ergonomically correct.
- Avoid clutter and stay organized. Don't create piles of papers and books on furniture and the floor. You won't be able to find anything and it's unpleasant working in a dirty, cluttered environment.
- Adjust your office furniture so that your monitor is just below eye level and at arm's length when you sit in your chair.
- Position your monitor so that glare from the sun or electric lights does not interfere with your ability to see the screen. Position your keyboard so that your fingers are below your wrists. Place gel pads in front of your keyboard and mouse to avoid placing pressure on the nerves of your wrists.
- Take regular breaks throughout the day. Stand up and stretch, flex your fingers and hands, and

take a quick walk around your office at least
once an hour.

Don't forget about making your clients comfortable too. If
you are meeting with your clients in your home office, keep the
following points in mind.

- Provide the clients with a comfortable chair in
  front of a desk or table where he or she can spread
  out materials and take notes with ease.
- Make sure that your office space is clean and neat.
- Offer a variety of beverages such as coffee, tea, and
  soft drinks. Have a supply of decaffeinated drinks
  as well.
- Have any documents prepared in advance so that
  you won't interrupt the meeting to make copies,
  gather materials, etc.
- Do not allow your children to attend or to
  interrupt meetings with your clients. These
  types of disruptions interfere with the focus of
  the meeting and may annoy your client. It does
  not give the impression of a serious business
  environment.
- Do not allow your pets to interrupt a meeting.
  Clients will probably not appreciate having a dog
  or cat jump on them, bark at them, or lick them.
  Remember that some clients may also be allergic to
  animals. Dust and vacuum your office before any
  meetings occur to eliminate animal hair and odors.

CONCLUSION

The home office is a tremendous asset to the nurse entrepreneur.
It allows the new small business owner freedom, flexibility, and
comfort. Your home office must enhance your image as a serious
business owner. You must establish and maintain this space as
an organized, neat, clean, professional place of business.

Your home office must be comfortable as well as functional.
Remember that it is a place of business and should be kept

separate from family activities. It is not an extension of your family room or living room. It is *your* space, designed to help you succeed as an entrepreneur.

RESOURCES

Drake, S. M. (2001). *Freelancing for Dummies.* New York: Hungry Minds.

Edwards, P., Edwards, S., & Economy, P. (2000). *Home-Based Business for Dummies.* Foster City, CA: IDG Books.

Hingston, P., & Balfour, A. (2001). *Working from Home.* New York: Dorling Kindersley.

Lesonsky, R. (2004). *Start Your Own Business.* Canada: Entrepreneur Press.

Appendix A:

Dos and Don'ts
for the Nurse Entrepreneur

Here are some simple statements that highlight the dos and don'ts of nursing entrepreneurship.

TEN STEPS FOR SUCCESS

Step One

Plan your journey as an entrepreneur carefully. Conduct your market research, calculate a budget, and understand the legal issues that impact businesses such as yours *before* you assume the role of full-time entrepreneur. If possible, start your entrepreneurial activities on a part-time basis while you still have the relative security of your "regular" full-time job. This allows a gradual transition to the role of business owner.

Step Two

Establish a serious business environment. Whether your office is in your home or in a downtown office building, make it look like the office of a successful entrepreneur. The image you, your employees, and your surroundings project is critical to your success.

Step Three

Maintain the skills and knowledge expected of a health care entrepreneur. If you are a continuing education consultant, keep your teaching skills and credentials up-to-date. If you are a management consultant, keep abreast of the latest management and leadership trends and expectations. Also stay current on medical advances, economic issues, and political events that impact health care delivery. If you are a clinical consultant, you must maintain your clinical skills.

Step Four

Love what you do. As an entrepreneur, you will work harder than you ever have, put in longer hours than you thought possible, and take greater risks than ever before. You must love your small business in order to meet these challenges.

Step Five

Conduct yourself professionally at all times. Just because you work from home and no one would actually *see* that you go barefoot while working at your computer is no reason to reduce your professional standards. Always present the image of a professional business owner. Never let your clients see you or hear you behave as anything else.

Step Six

Present a self-confident image. As an entrepreneur you are always in position to "sell" yourself and your products and services to strangers. If you don't have confidence in yourself, neither will your clients.

Step Seven

Never charge less than what you're worth. Learn to negotiate and to compromise but never accept a fee you know is unfair.

Step Eight

Plan vacation and leisure time and take it! Take time to rest, enjoy life, and "recharge" your professional batteries.

Step Nine

Save a designated amount of money, no matter how small, from each paycheck. You'll be glad you did when business is slow, and nearly all entrepreneurs experience tough times.

Step Ten

Always do your best work, and don't forget to reward yourself! After the completion of an exceptionally successful project do something your really enjoy! Take an afternoon off just for yourself, play with the children, etc. Reward yourself with an inexpensive, but personally valued, "bonus."

TEN STEPS TO TAKE WHEN BUSINESS IS SLOW

Step One

Don't give up. Everyone experiences tough times. Count on the support of family, friends, colleagues, and your own belief that times will get better!

Step Two

Manage your cash flow carefully. Economize wherever possible.

Step Three

Accept temporary or part-time work. This ensures a certain amount of income while allowing you time to generate business.

Step Four

Publish and/or present professional papers. A good way to advertise your business is by publishing articles in professional journals and presenting papers at professional association conventions and conferences.

Step Five

Volunteer your services. Hospitals, nursing homes, senior citizens centers etc., all need volunteers. This is a way to meet potential clients and network.

Step Six

Keep in touch with former clients and your network of entrepreneurs. They may be quite helpful in locating referrals for you.

Step Seven

Pursue payment from clients who owe you money. This is the time to be firm about receiving payments.

Step Eight

Offer special marketing promotions. For example, offer a 10% discount on services during a particular month of the year or a 15% discount if clients purchase a designated, significant number of products and services.

Step Nine

Don't sit in your office and mope. Network, publish, market, etc.

Step Ten

Don't take out your frustration on family and friends. You need them more than ever during tough times. And when business improves don't forget to reward them for their encouragement and support

TEN THINGS *NOT* TO DO

Don't become an entrepreneur just because you're unhappy with your current employer. While adverse working conditions may well be a reason for you to look for another job, they are not necessarily a reason to start your own business.

Don't become an entrepreneur because you are looking for job security or want to work fewer hours. Small businesses often fail. Success requires planning, hard work, and long hours. And remember, entrepreneurship carries a significant amount of risk.

Never use your bedroom as your home office. Your ability to relax is compromised because your work infringes on your most intimate space.

Don't procrastinate. A new entrepreneur may encounter many distractions, especially if he or she works from home. Minimize distractions and don't put off unpleasant or boring tasks.

Don't let your home office become an extension of your family's space. Your home office must be maintained as a professional business environment.

Don't count on a larger income right away! Set realistic goals concerning revenue and expenses.

Don't rely on one client for the majority of your income. Diversify your clientele.

Don't burn bridges. Resign from your "regular" jobs on good terms with your employer. Don't "bad mouth" clients, and be sure to avoid any appearance of conflict of interest.

Don't "forget" a client once a project is completed. Keep in touch with former clients. They may have more work for you in the future and are a good source of referrals.

Don't work all the time. You need to "end" your work day. If you work all of the time you will jeopardize your health, your interpersonal relationships, and your productivity.

RESOURCES

Allen, K. (2001). *Entrepreneurship for Dummies.* New York: Wiley Publishing.

Drake, S. M. (2001). *Freelancing for Dummies.* New York: Hungry Minds.

Edwards, P., Edwards, S., & Economy, P. (2000). *Home-Based Business for Dummies.* Foster City, CA: IDG Books.

Hingston, P., & Balfour, A. (2001). *Working from Home.* New York: Dorling   Kindersley.

Lesonsky, R. (2004). *Start Your Own Business.* Canada: Entrepreneur Press.

Appendix B:
Useful Web Sites

Here is an alphabetical listing of the Web sites mentioned throughout this book for your quick reference. However, Web sites come and go rapidly. These sites were up and running at the time of publication.

American Association for Public Opinion Research:
   www.aapor.org
American Demographics: **www.demographics.com**
American Medical Writers Association: **www.amwa.org**
American Small Business Association: **www.asbaonline.org**

Business Wire: **www.businesswire.com**

Chamber of Commerce: **www.chamberofcommerce.com**
Copyright Office of the Library of Congress:
   www.loc.gov/copyright

Entrepreneur.Com: **www.entrepreneur.com**

Health Data Insights: **www.healthmarketinsights.com**
Hoover's Online: **www.hoovers.com**

Inc500: **www.Inc.com**

Internet Yellow Pages: **www.switchboard.com** or
    www.infospace.com

Le Tip: **www.letip.com**

National Nurses in Business Association (NNBA):
    www.nnba.net 1-877-353-8888

National Nursing Staff Development Organization:
    www.nnsdo.org

News Directory: **www.newsdirectory.com**

Nurse Entrepreneur Network:
    www.nurse-entrepreneur-network.org

ProfNet. **www.profnet.com**

Public Register's Annual Report Service: **www.prars.com**

Service Corps of Retired Executives: **www.score.org**

Small Business Administration: **www.sba.gov**

United States Census Bureau: **www.census.gov**

United States Chamber of Commerce: **www.uschamber.com**

United States Patent and Trademark Office: **www.uspto.gov**

United States Securities and Exchange Commission:
    www.sec.gov

Web Side Story: **www.websidestory.com**

Index

80/20 rule, 113

A

B

visualization, 34. *see also* entrepreneur;
    mind/body wellness

W

web design, 5. *see also* entrepreneur

Web Side Story, 124

work redesign, 22–23, 37–38. *see also*
    consultant; entrepreneur
    consultation specialty in, 22–23
    entrepreneurial service provision in,
        37–38

written agreements. *see* contracts

Y

yoga, 34. *see also* entrepreneur; mind/
    body wellness

Z

zoning regulations, 34, 72–76, 148. *see
    also* legal frameworks; licensure